ADULT COLORING BOOKS

I0513646

Butterfly EDEN

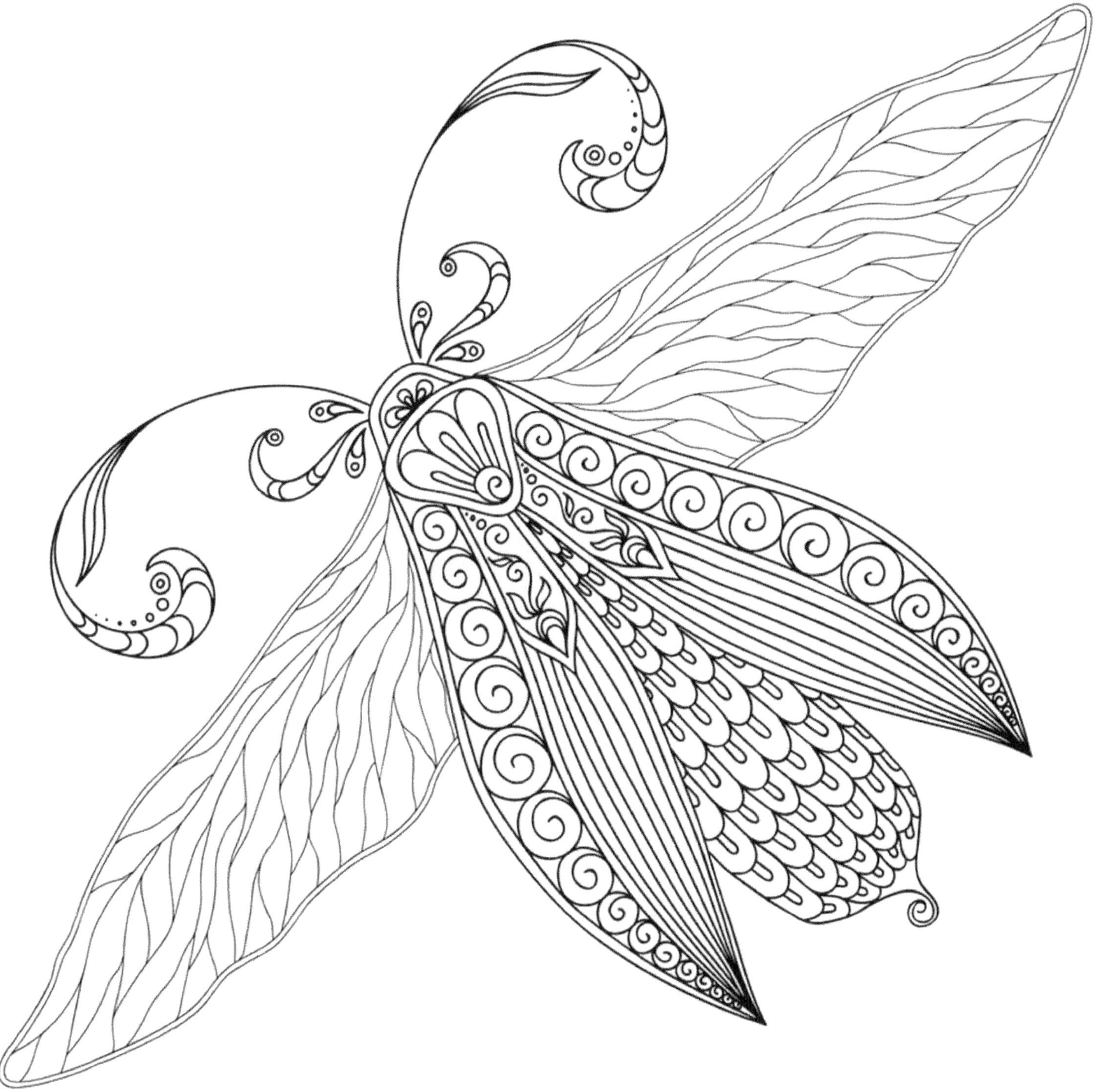

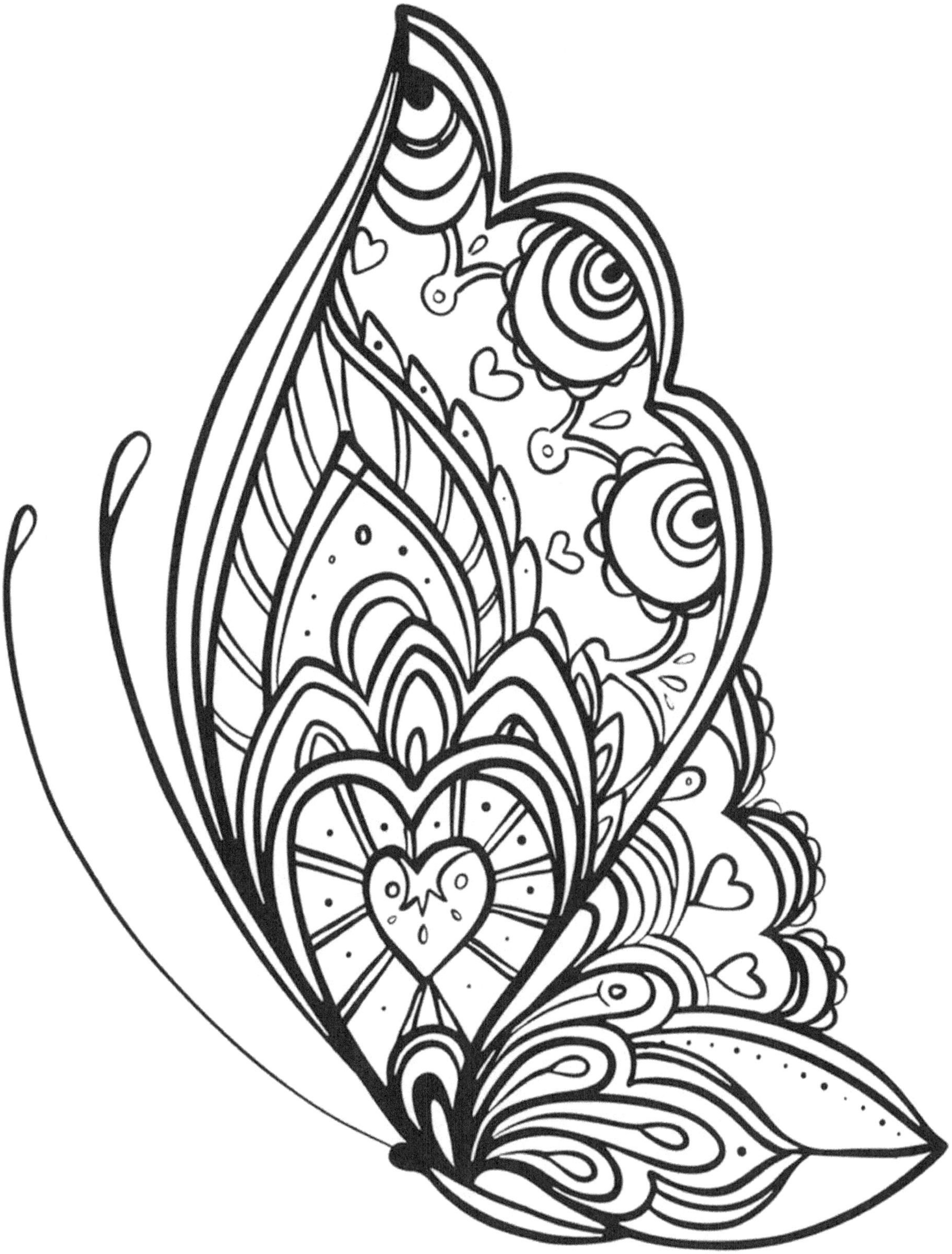

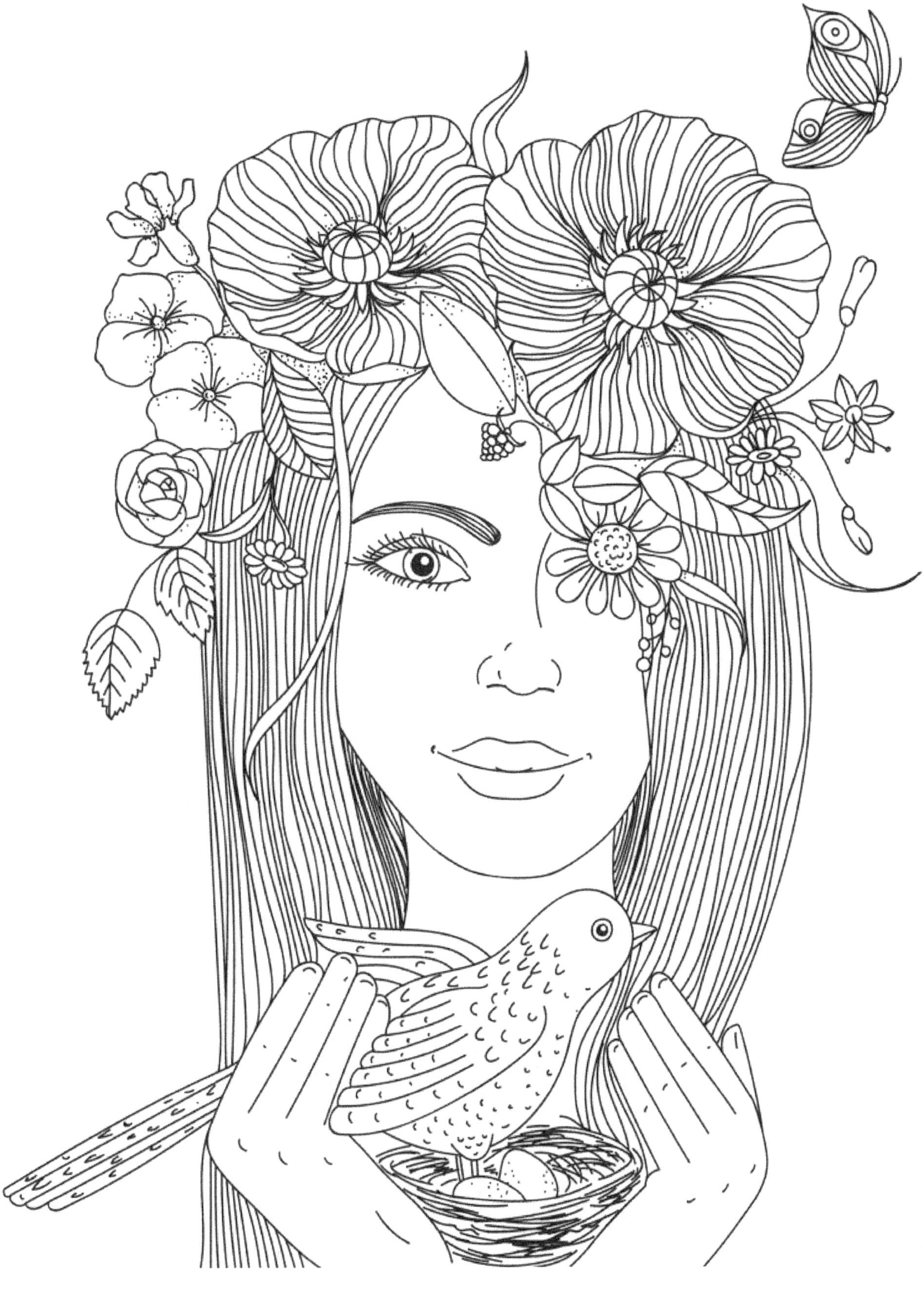

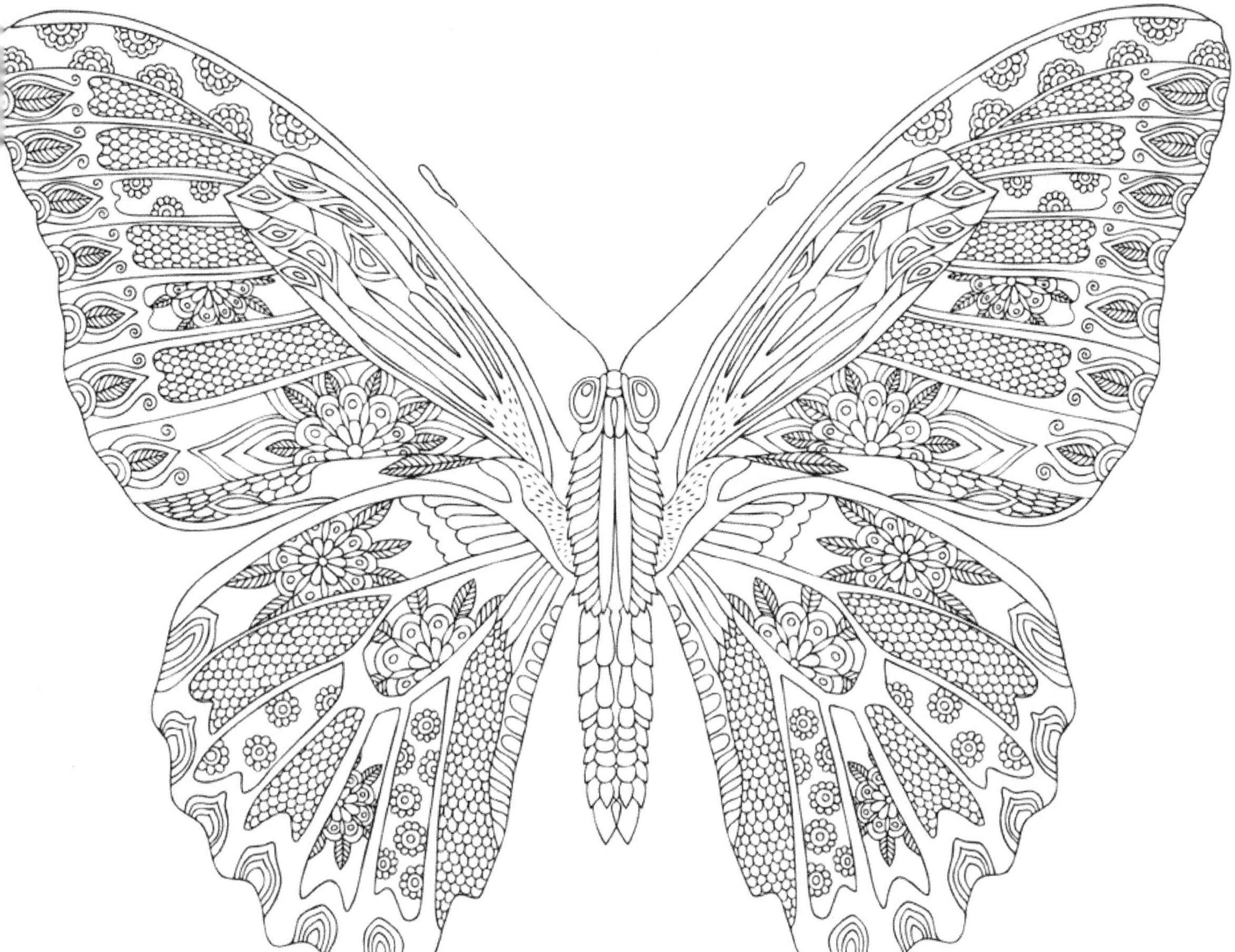

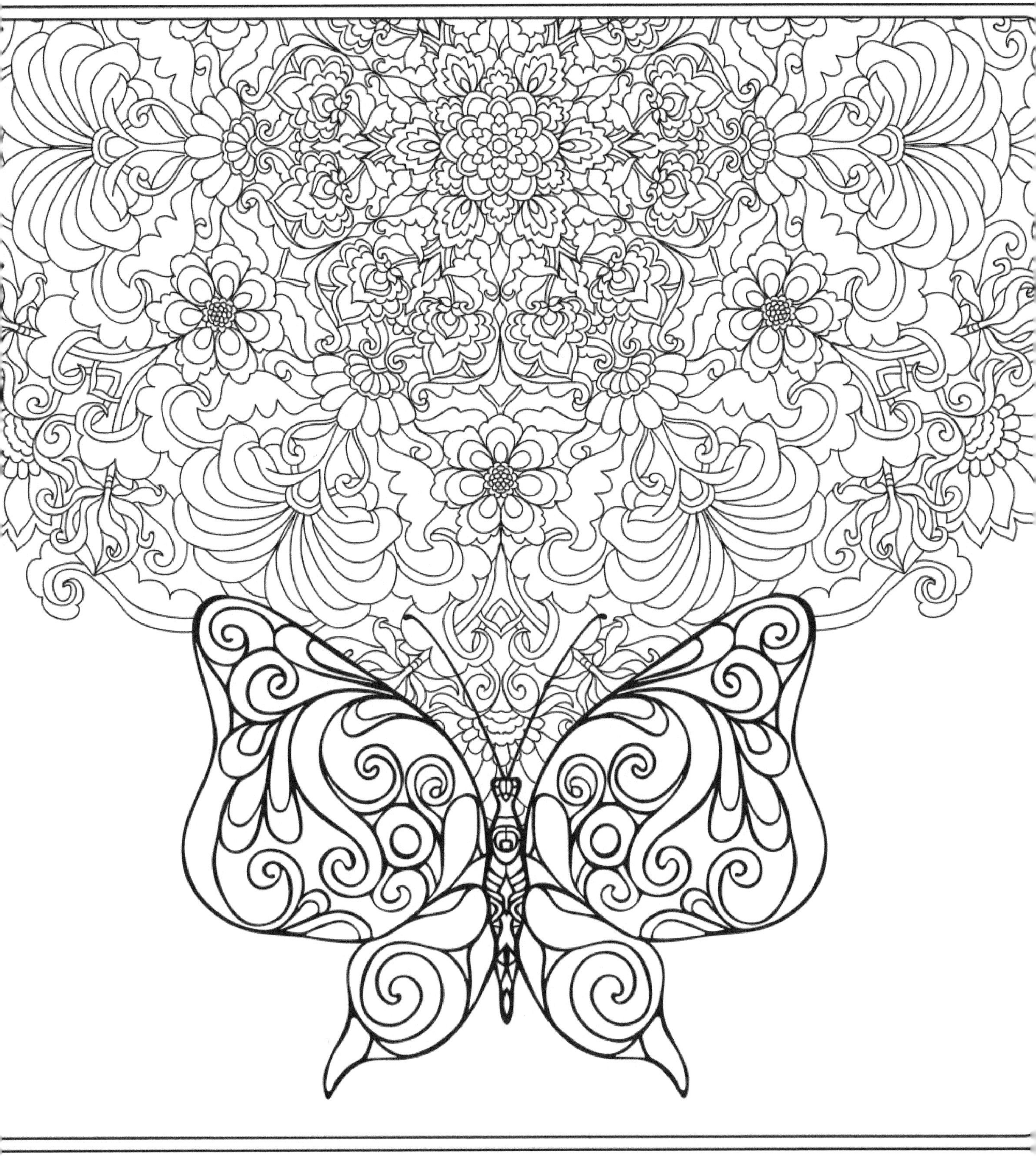

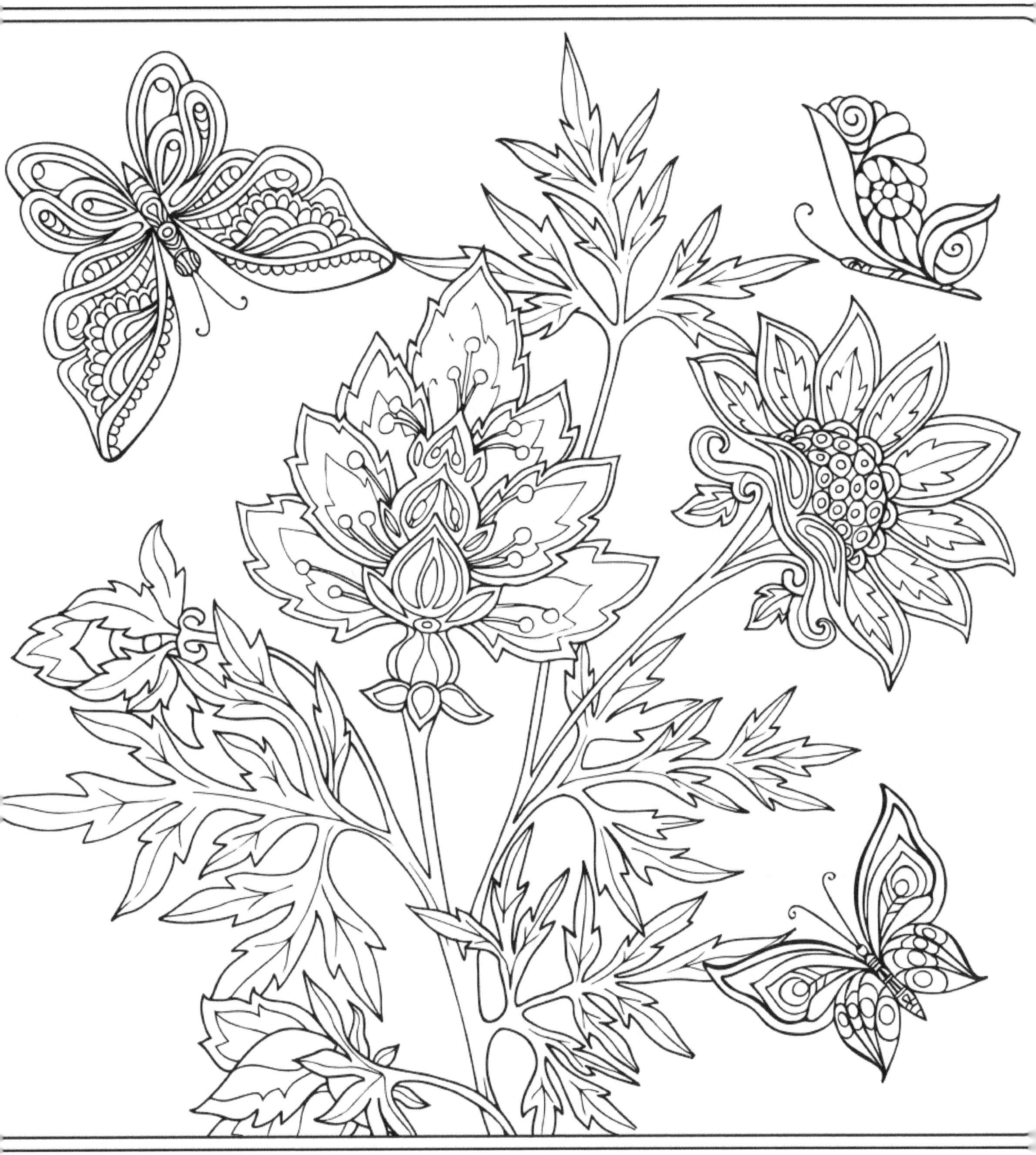

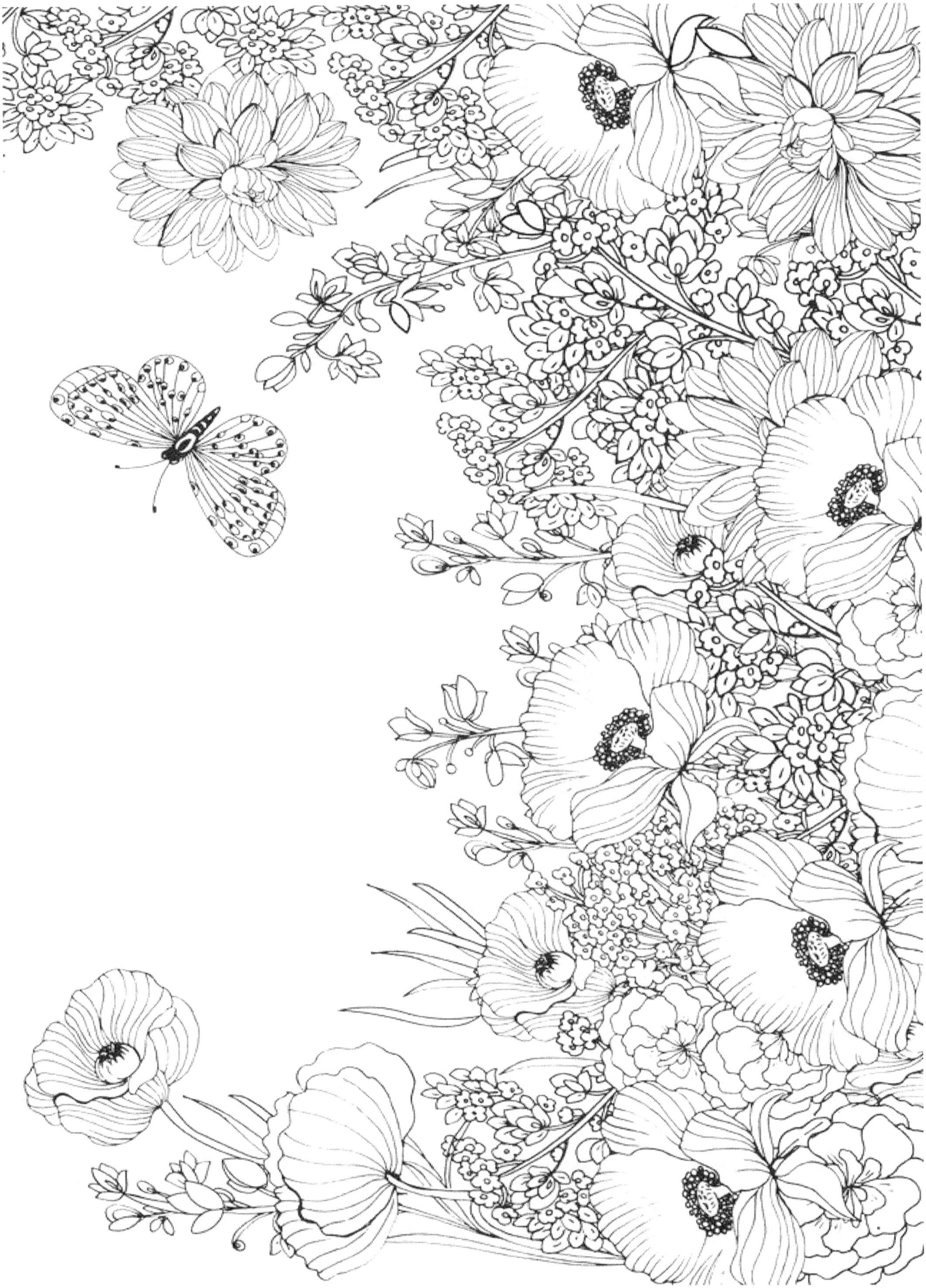

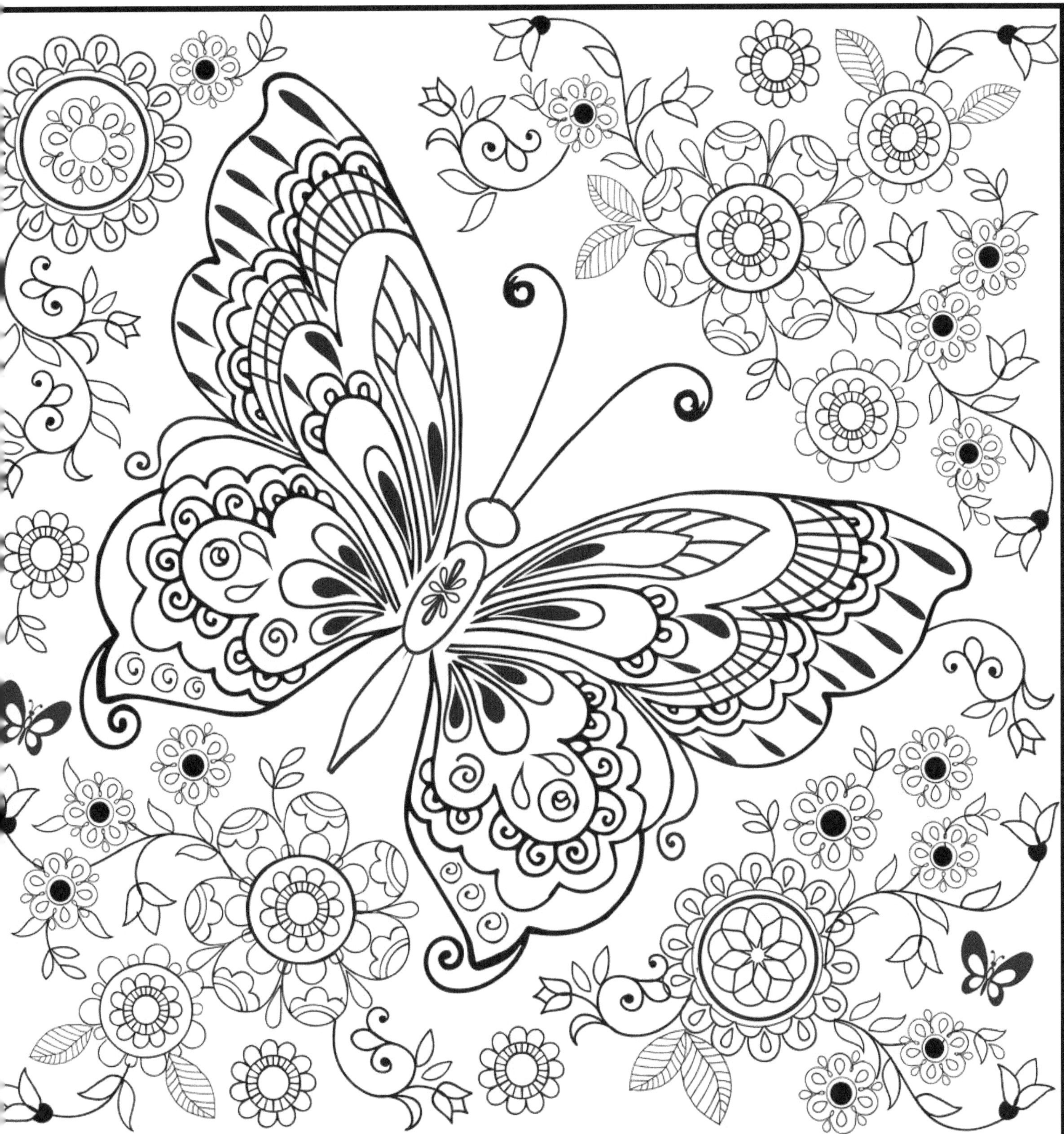

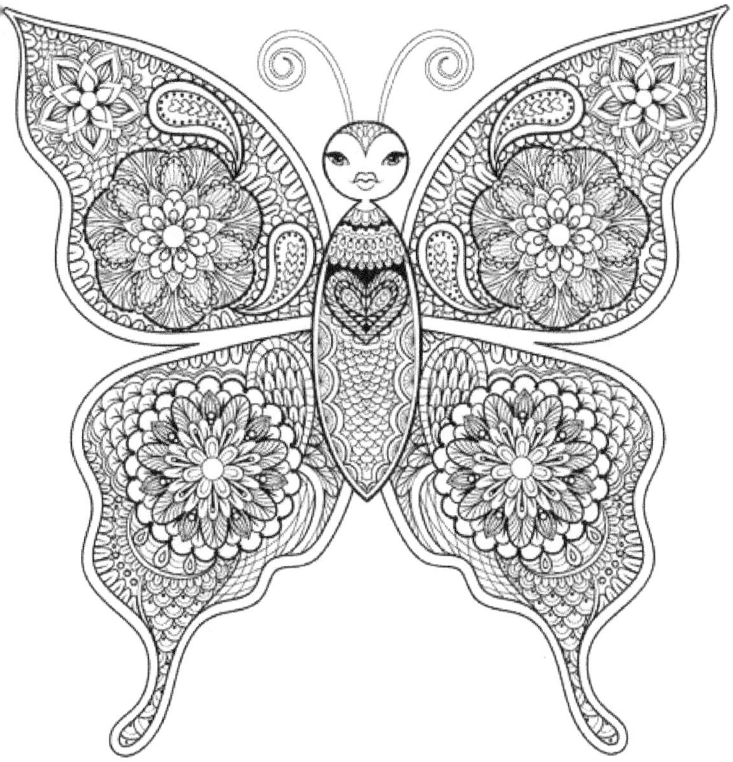
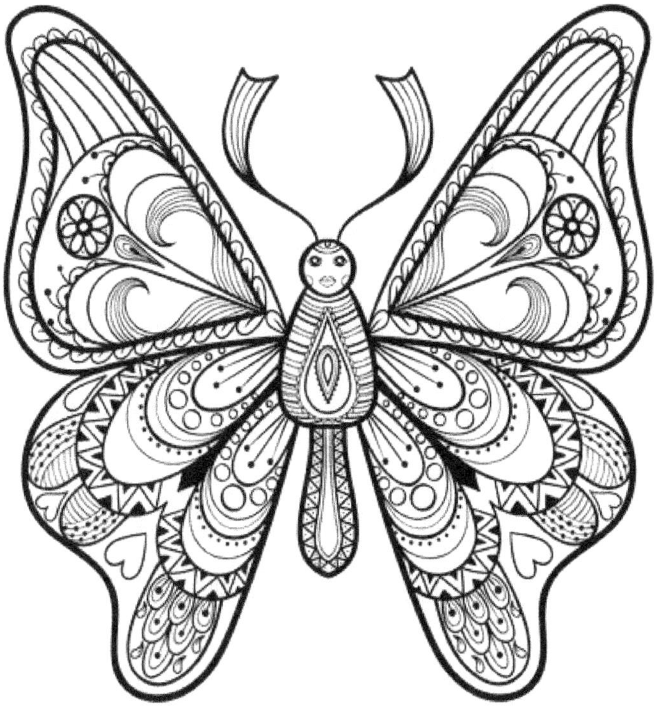
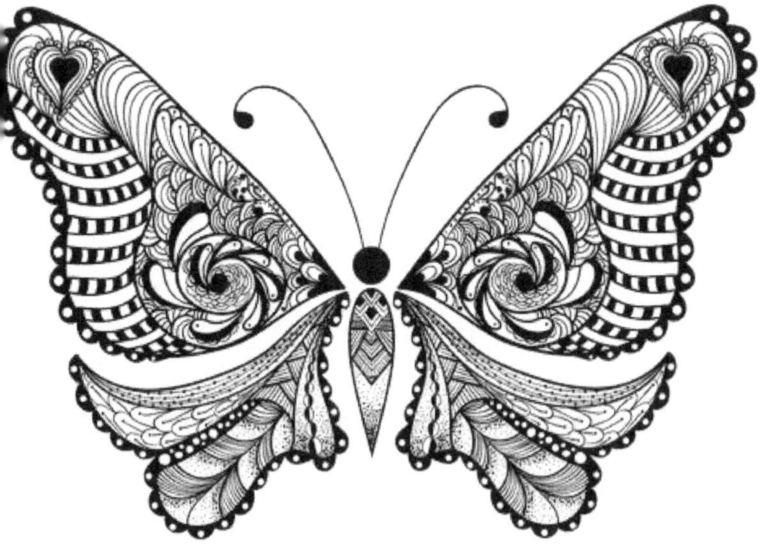
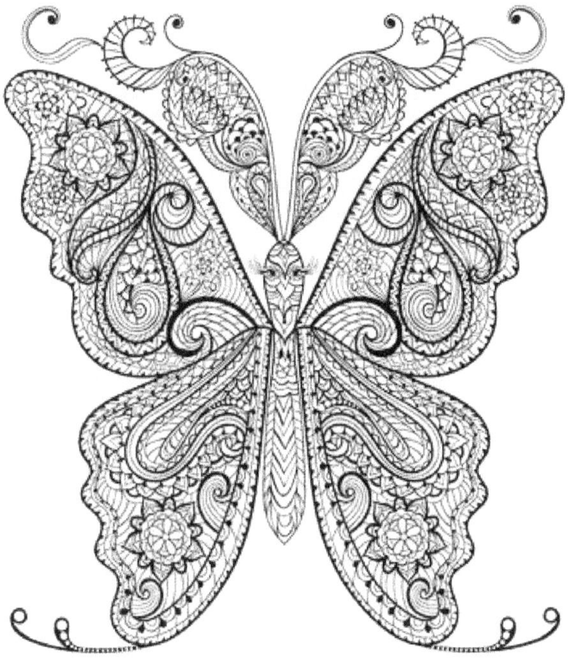

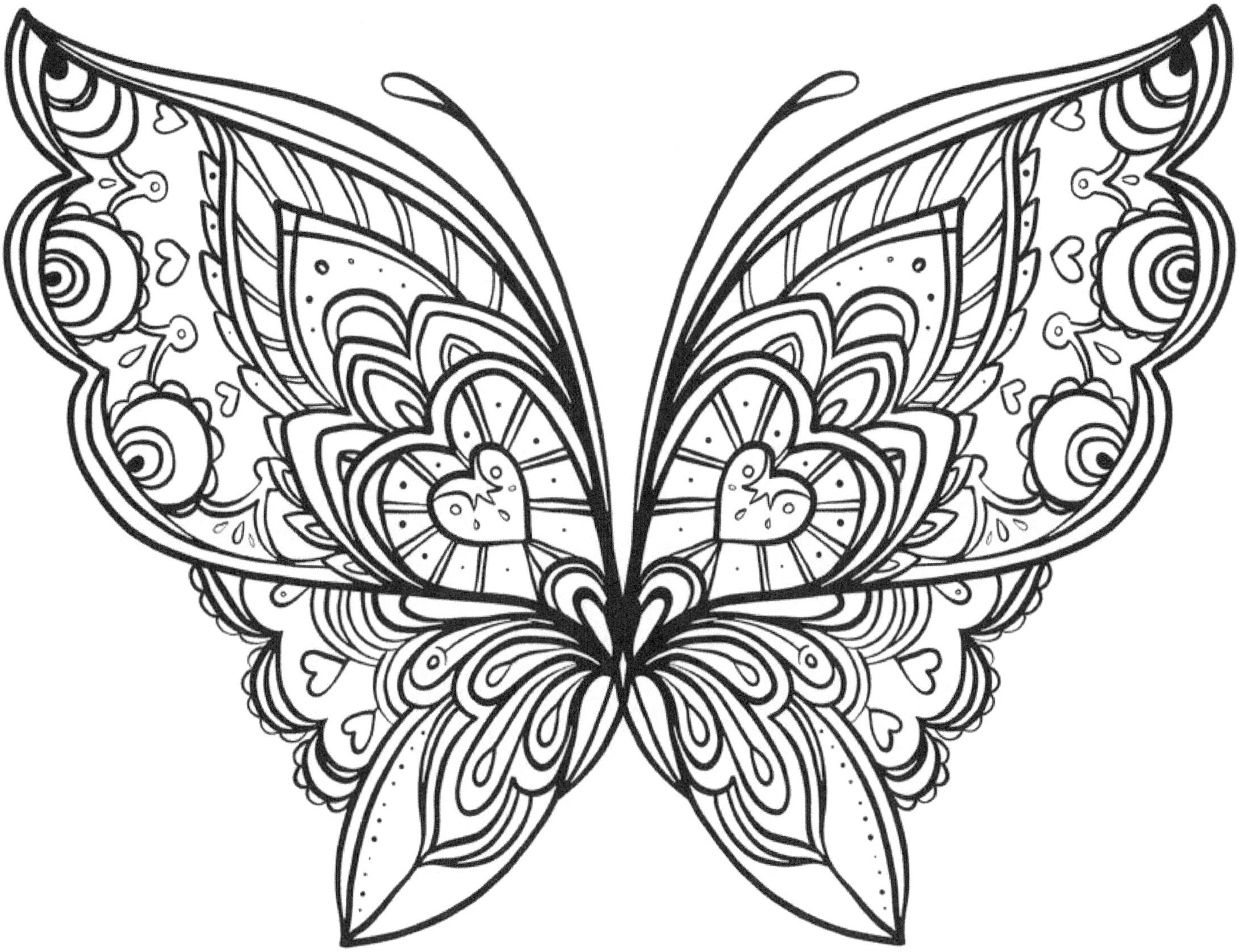

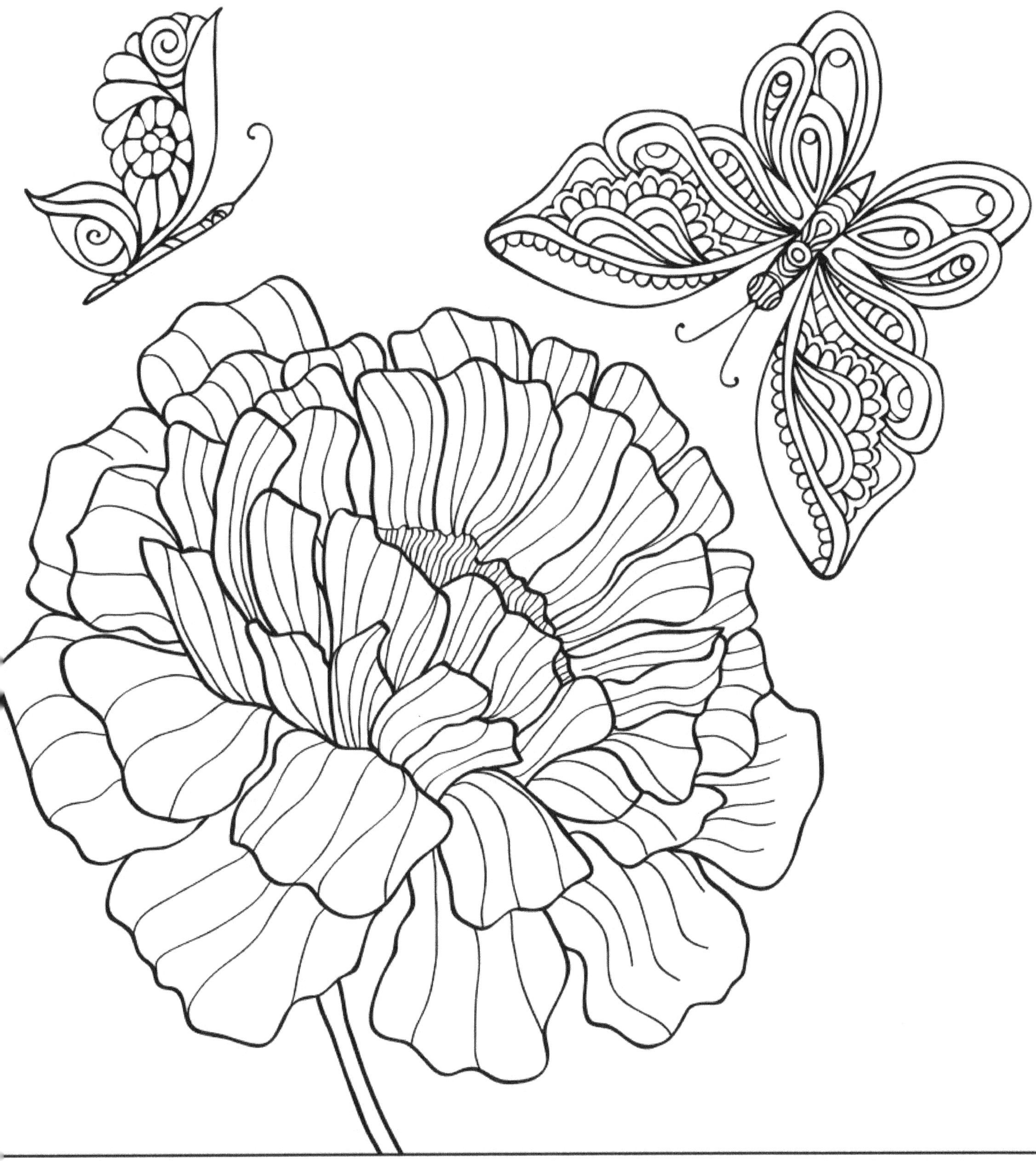

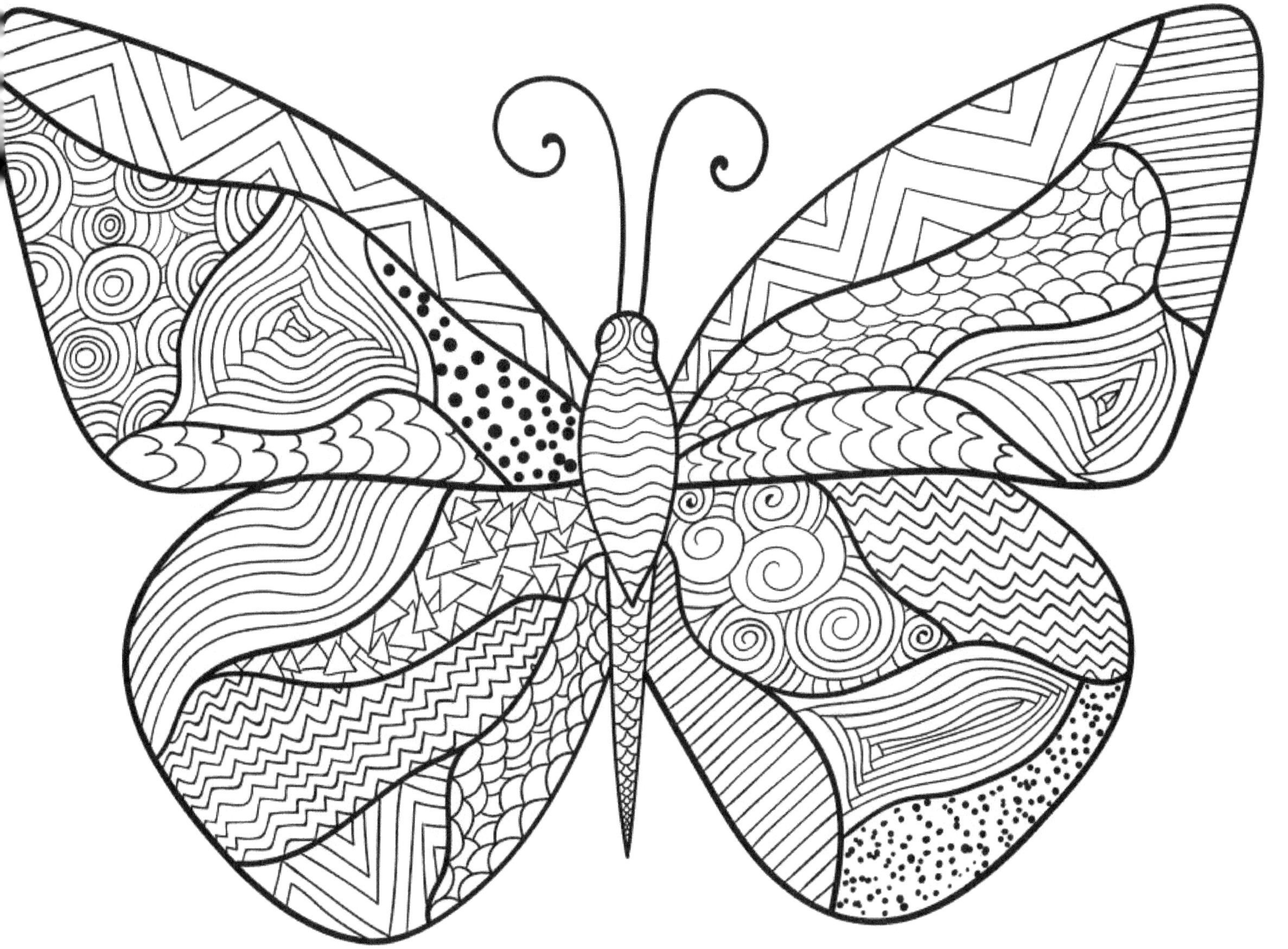

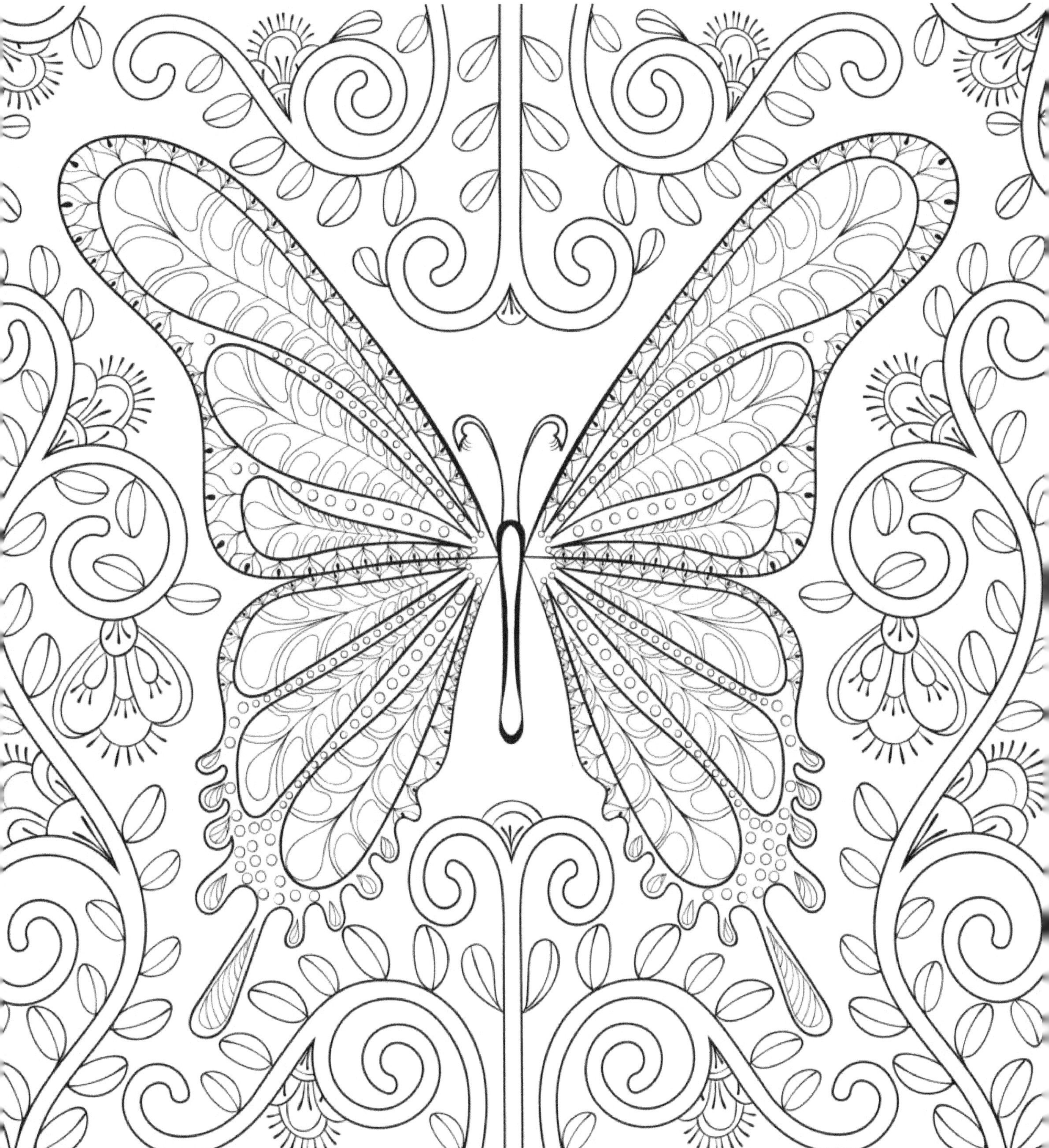

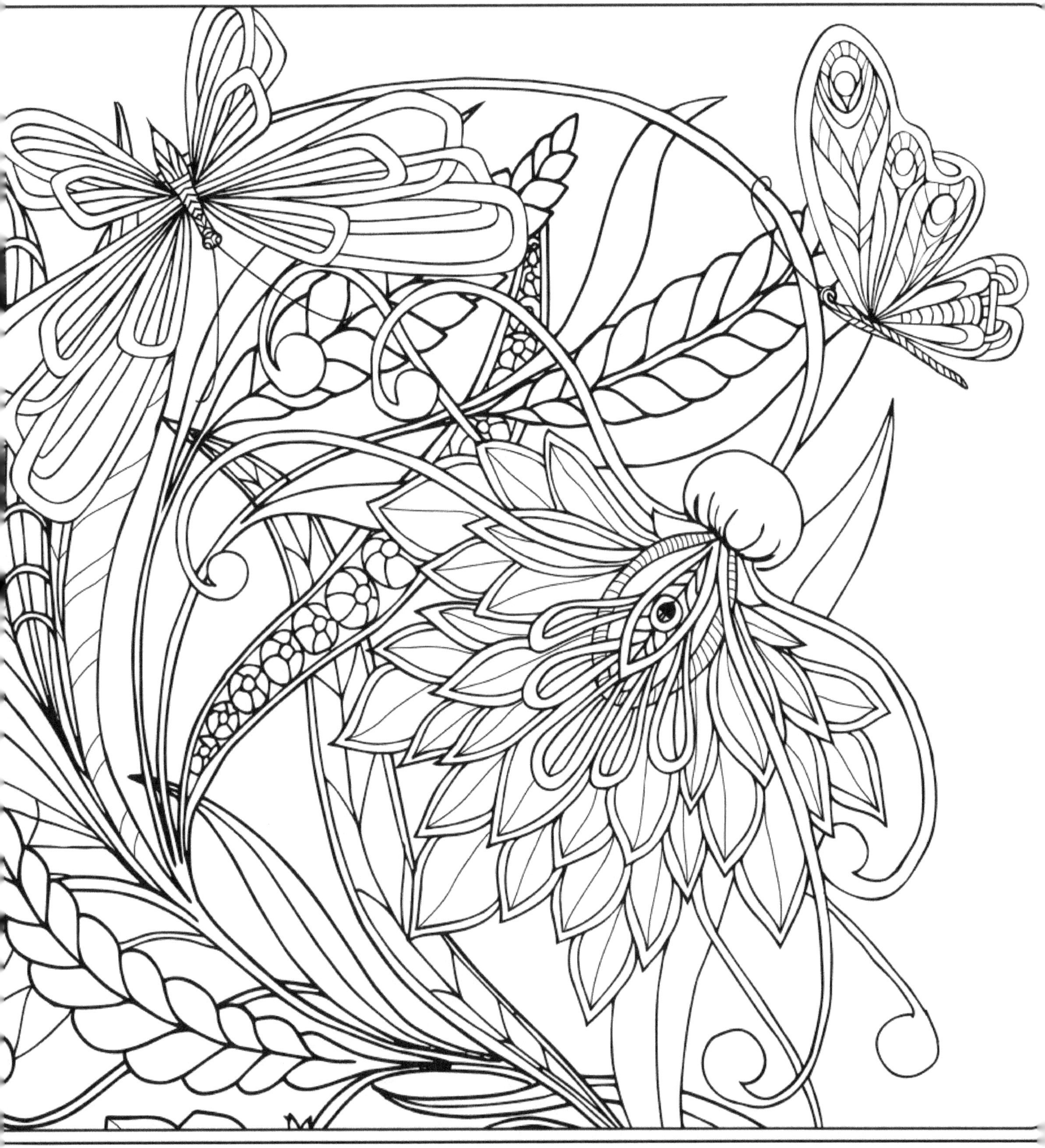

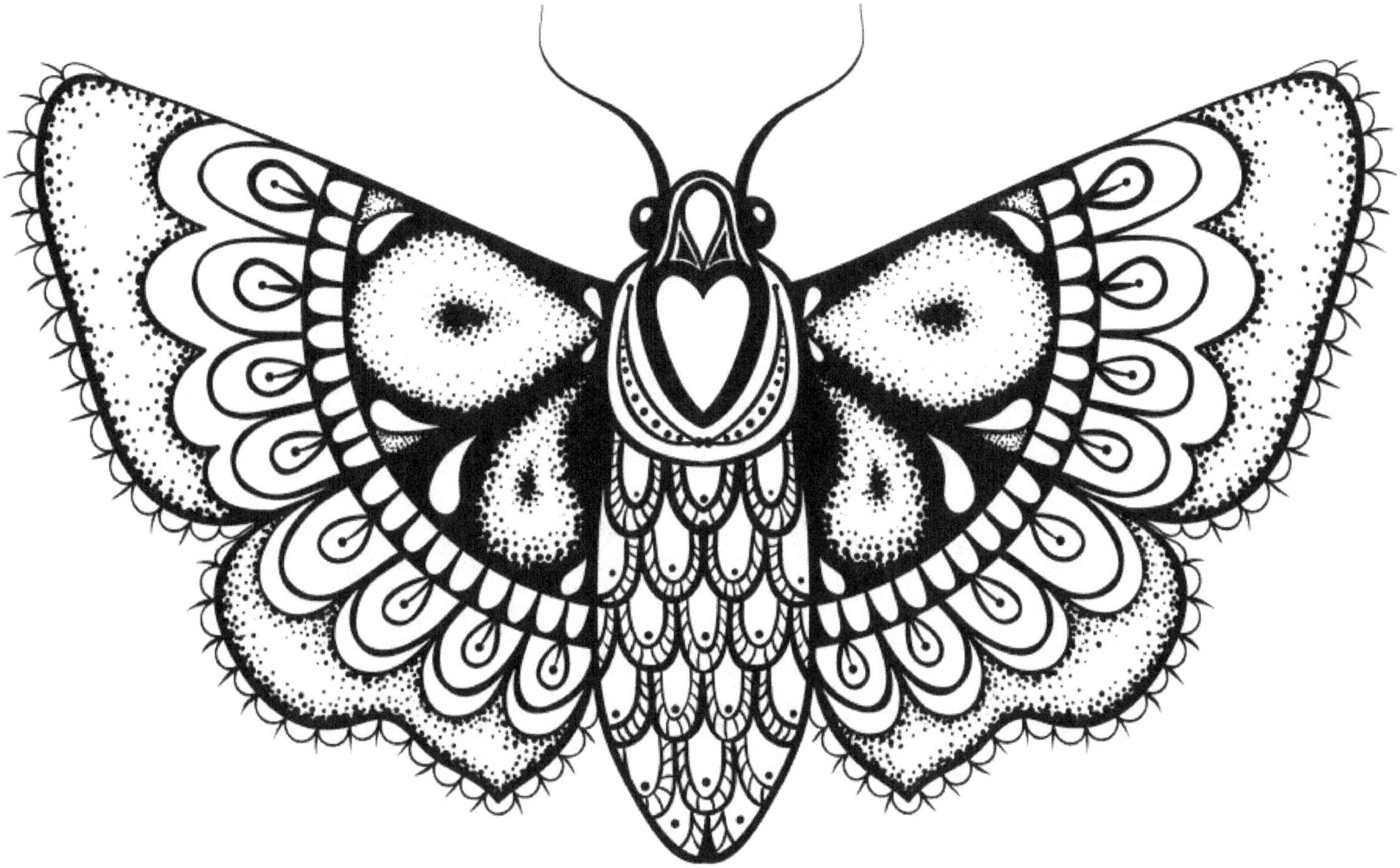

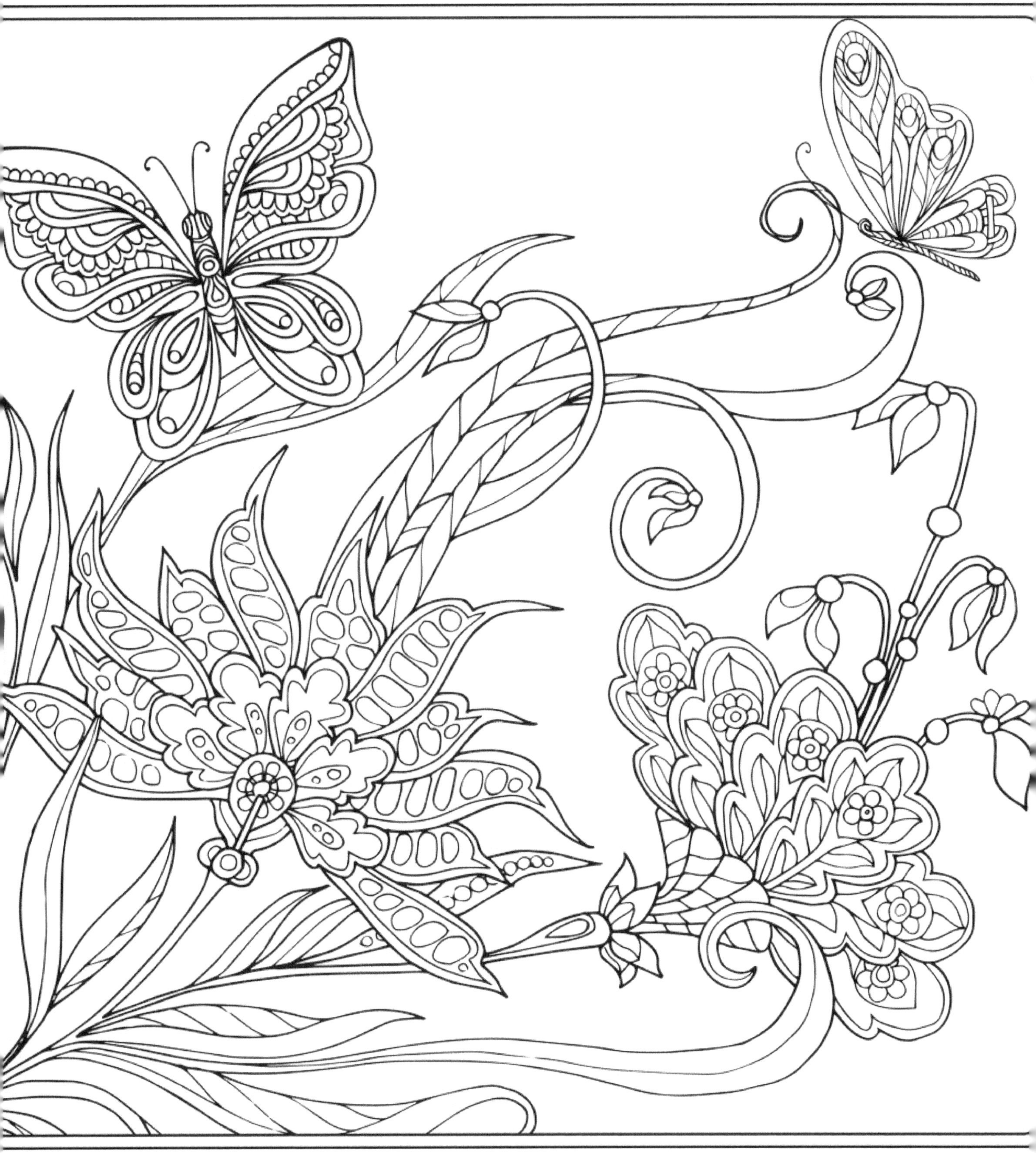

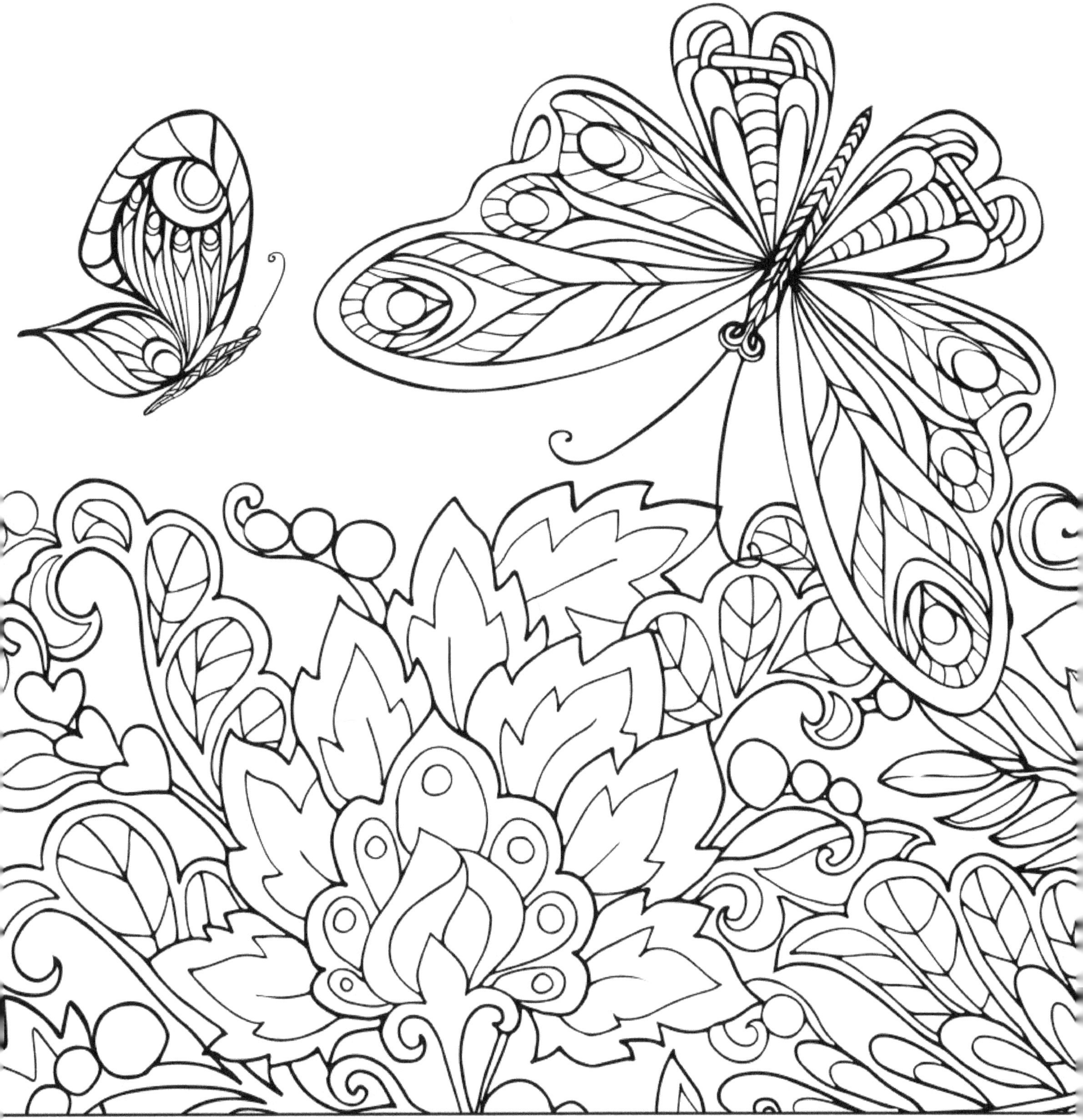

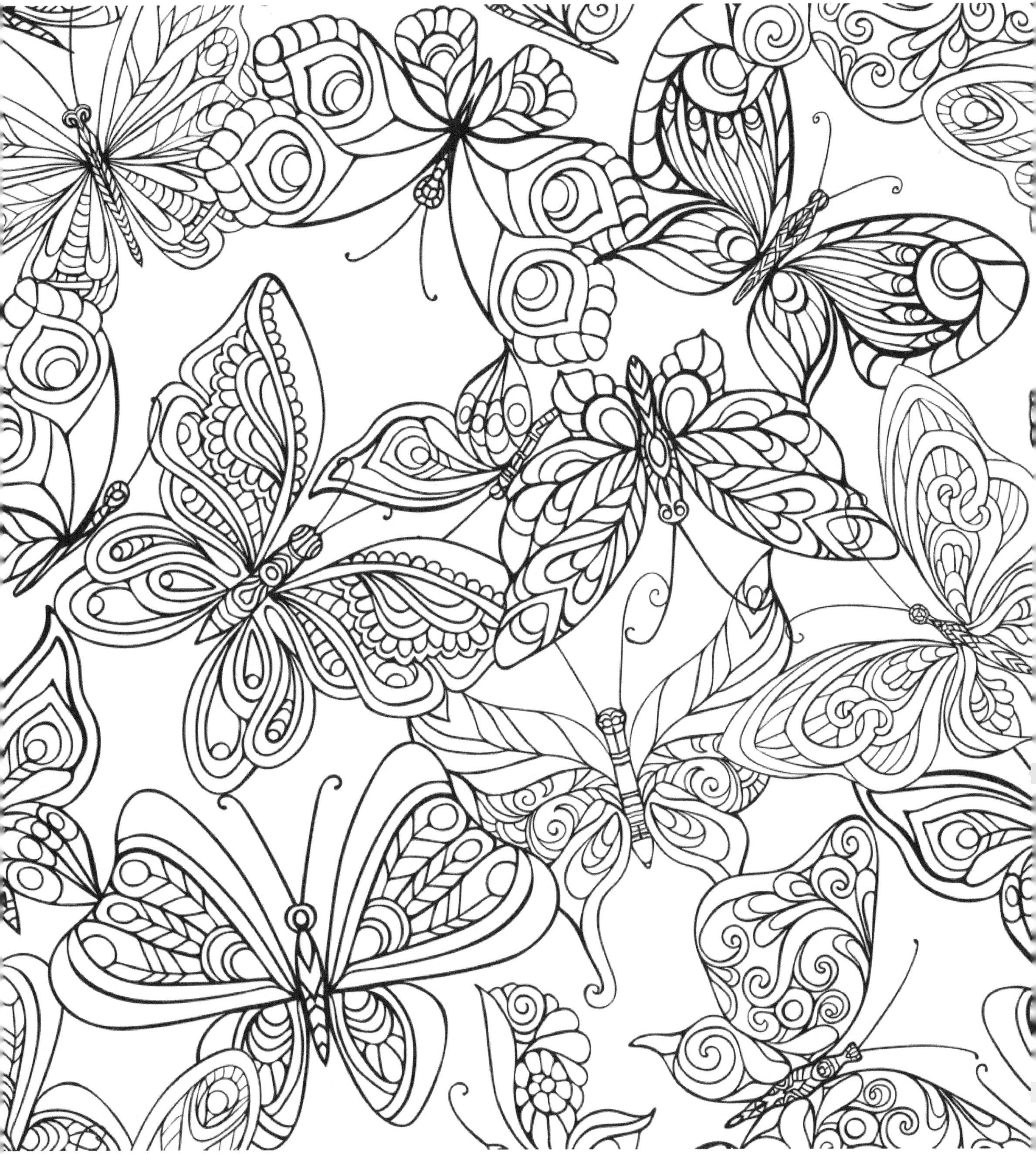

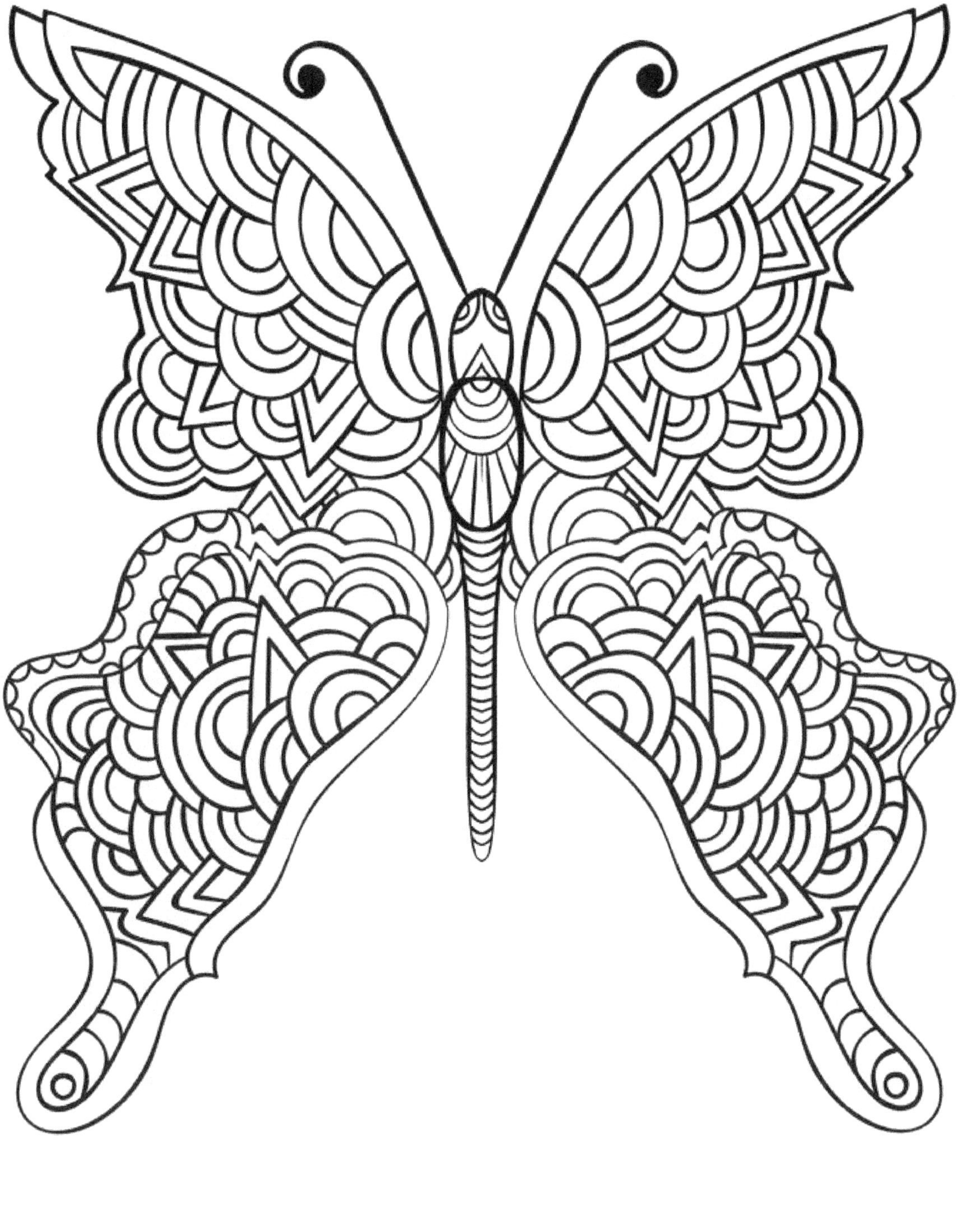

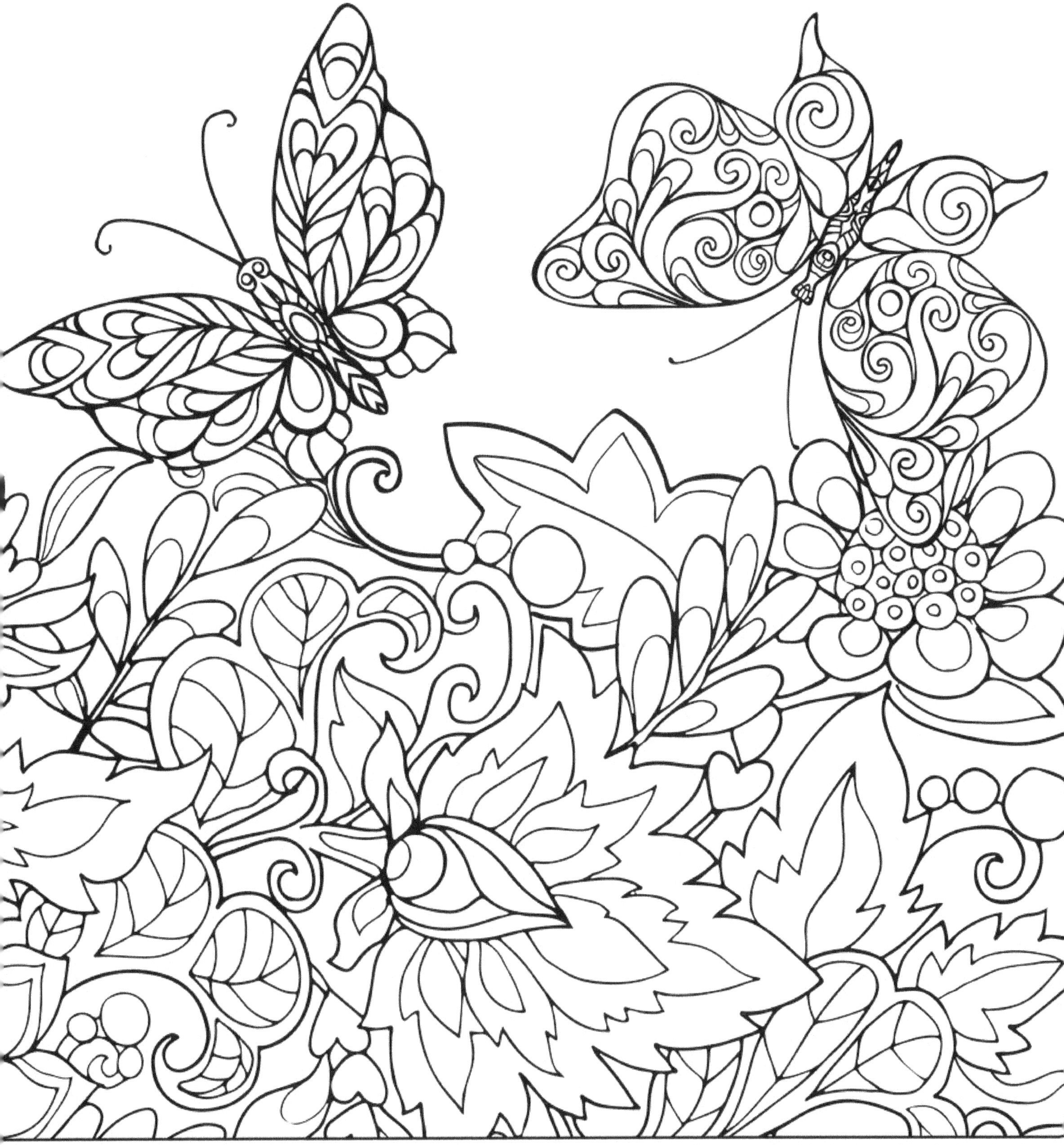

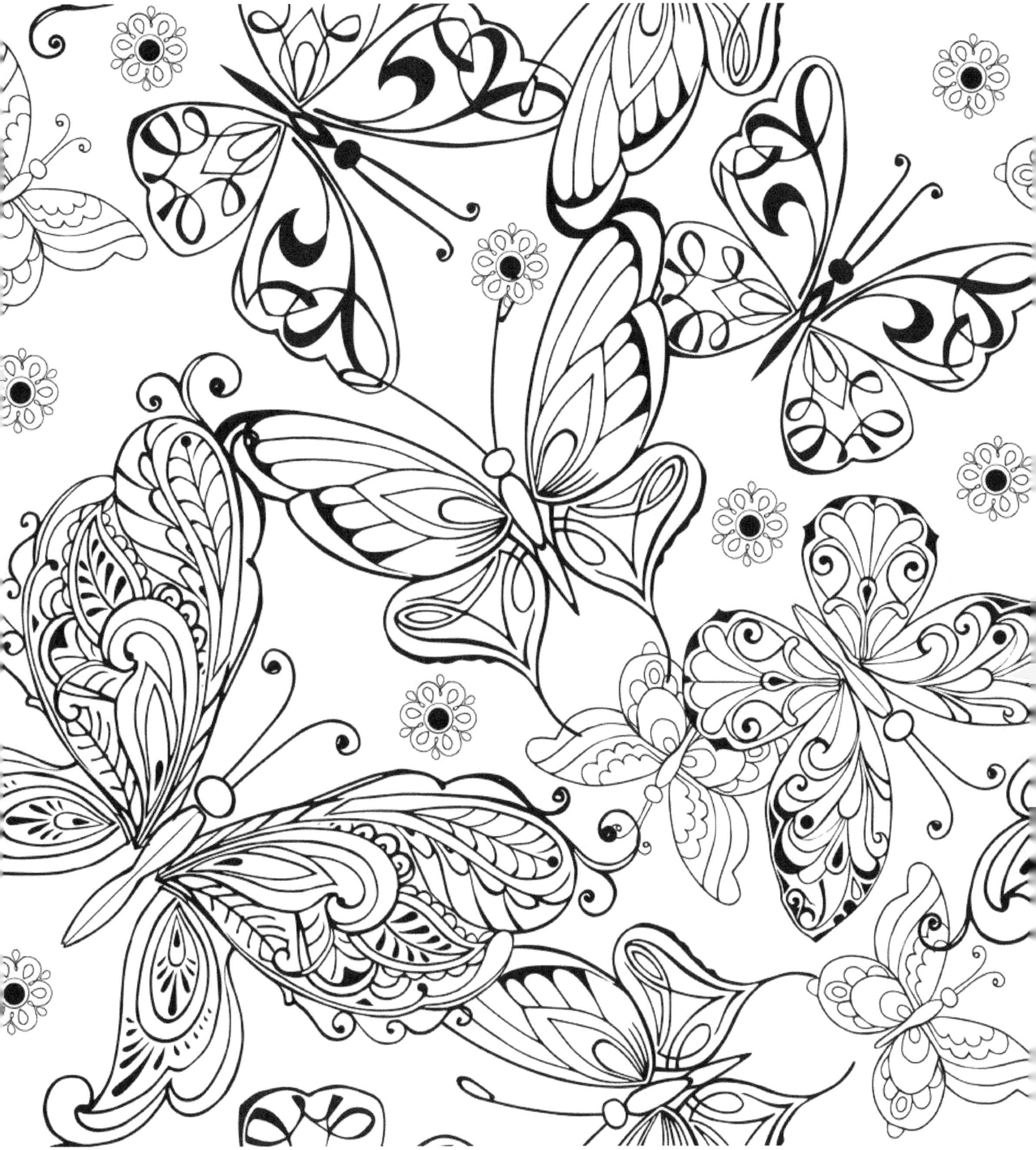

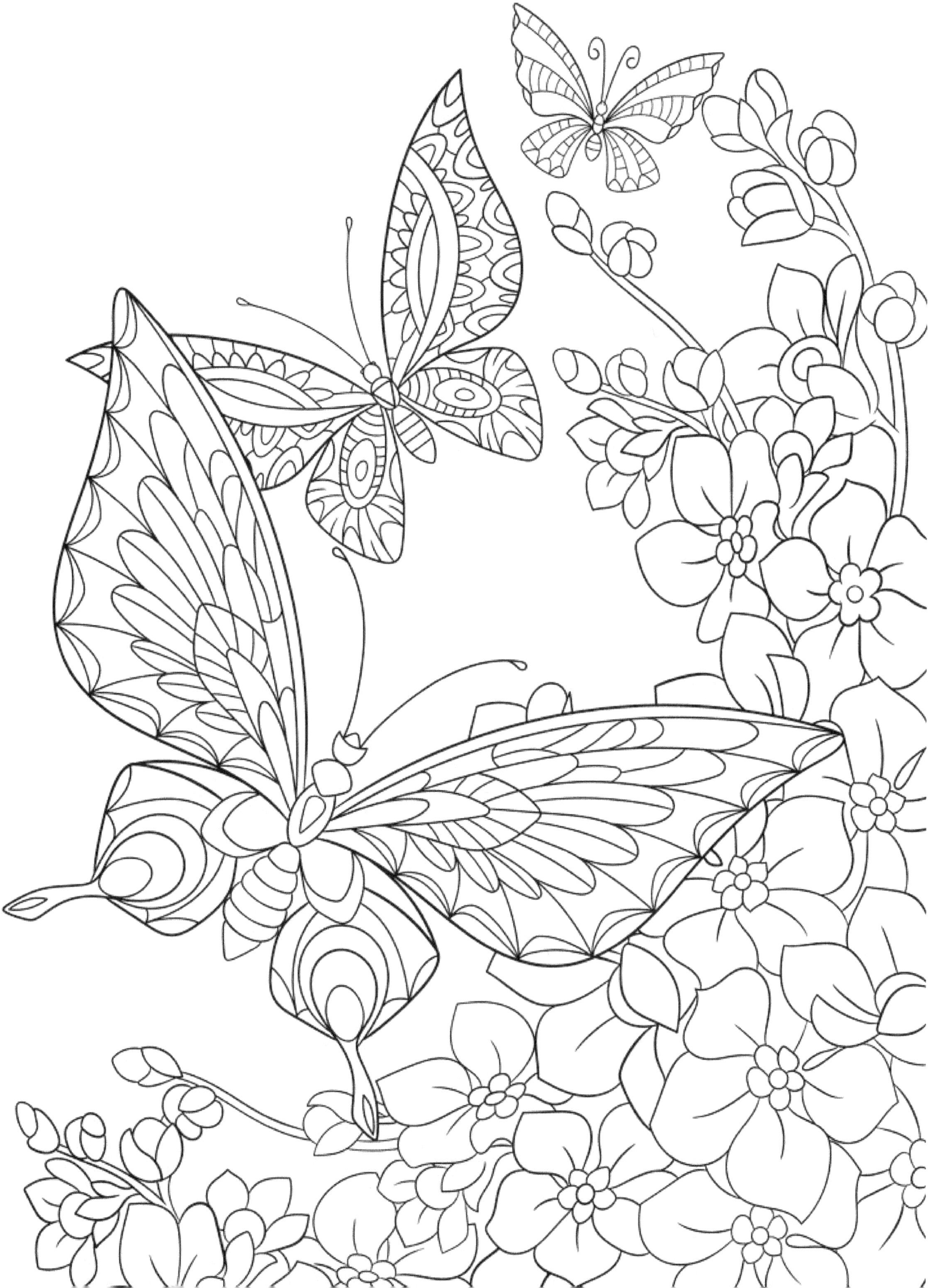

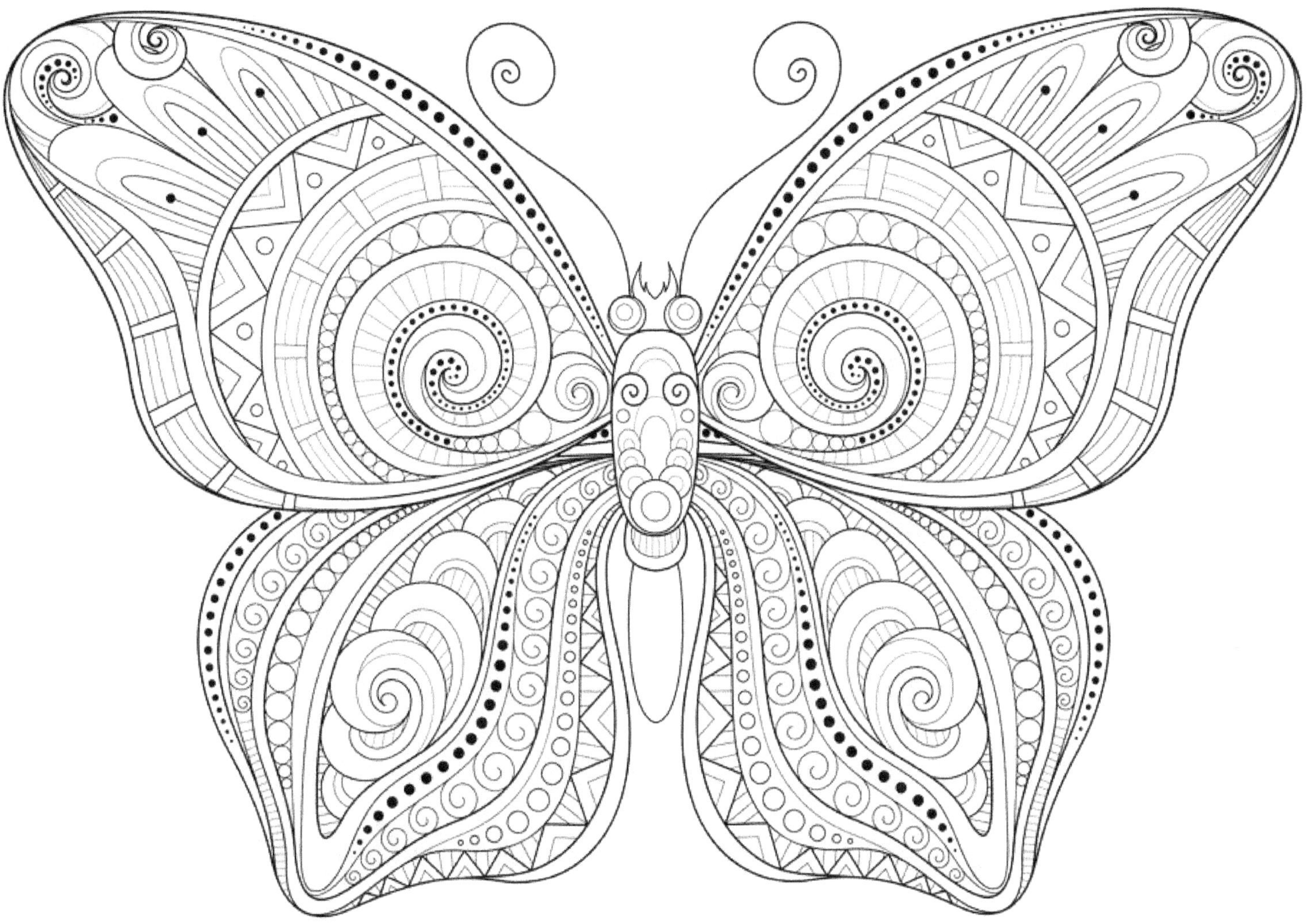

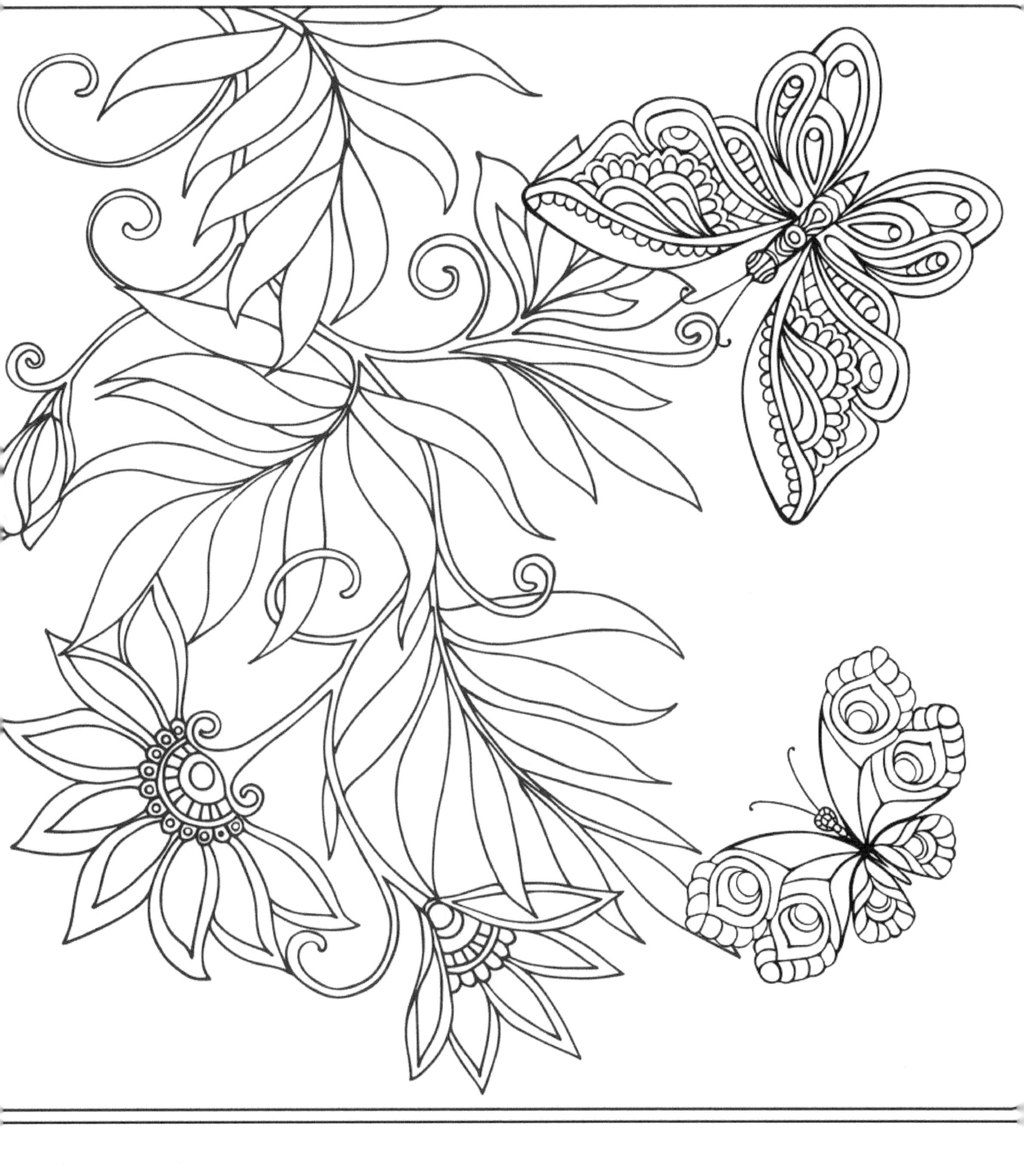

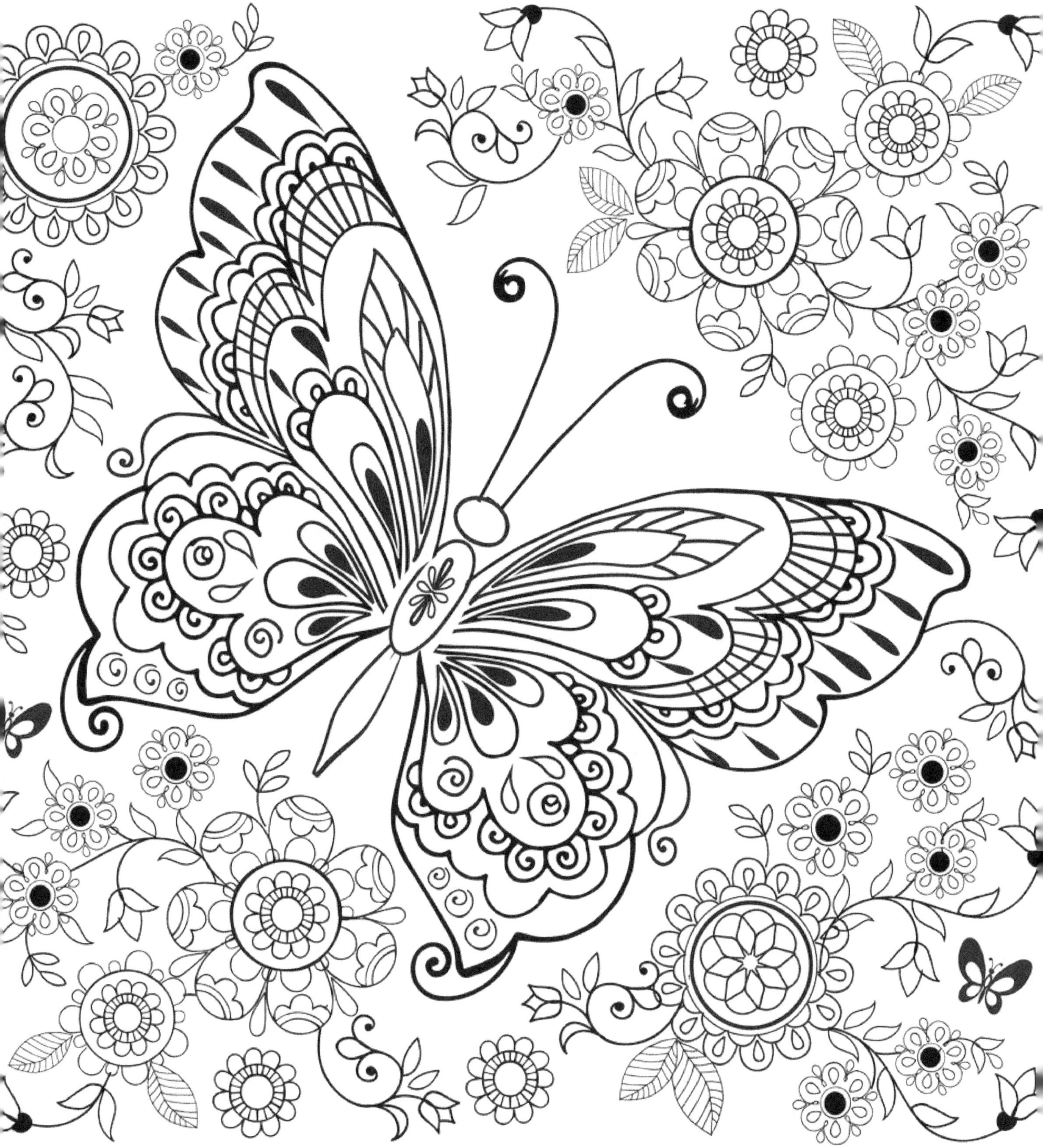

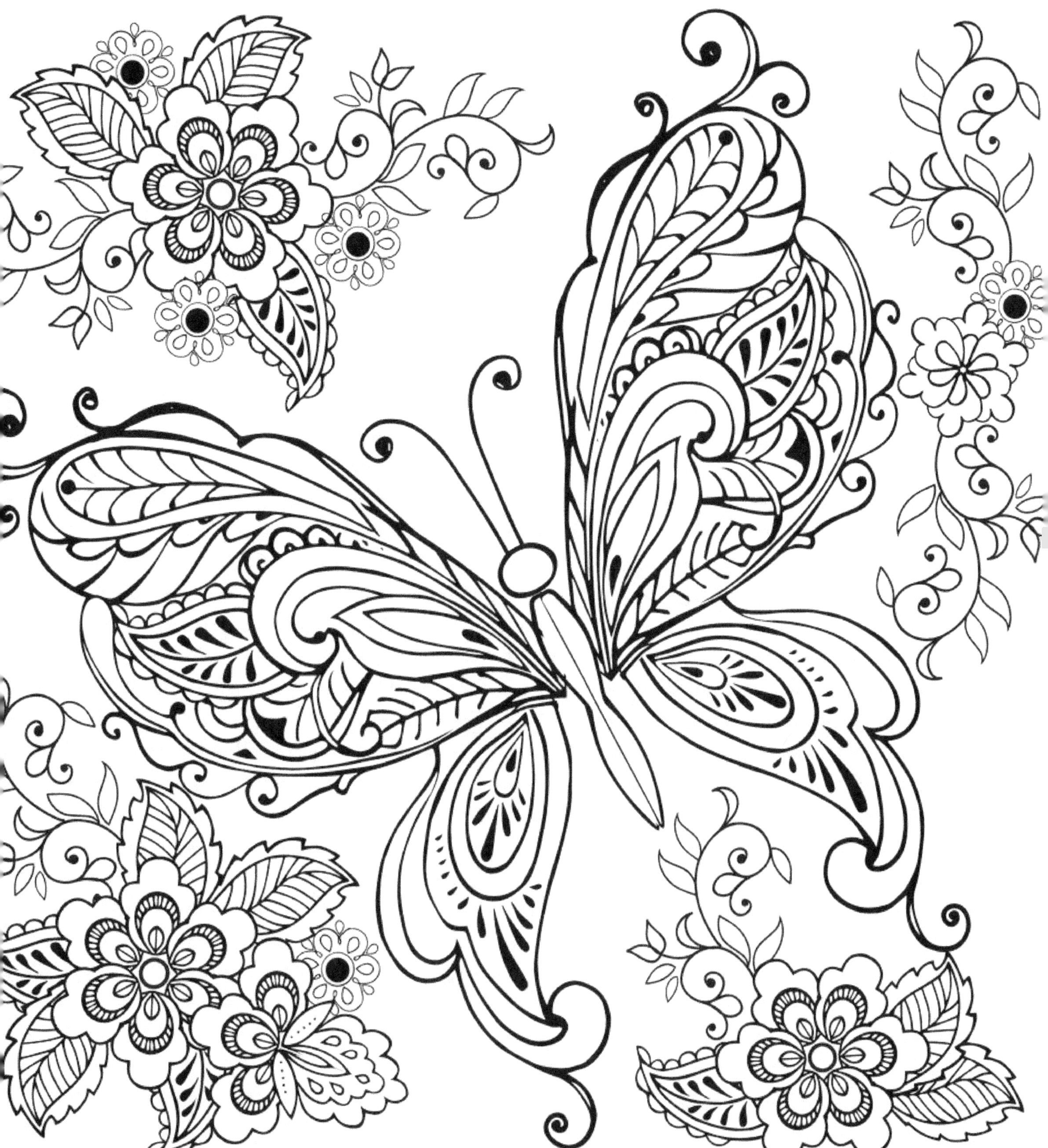

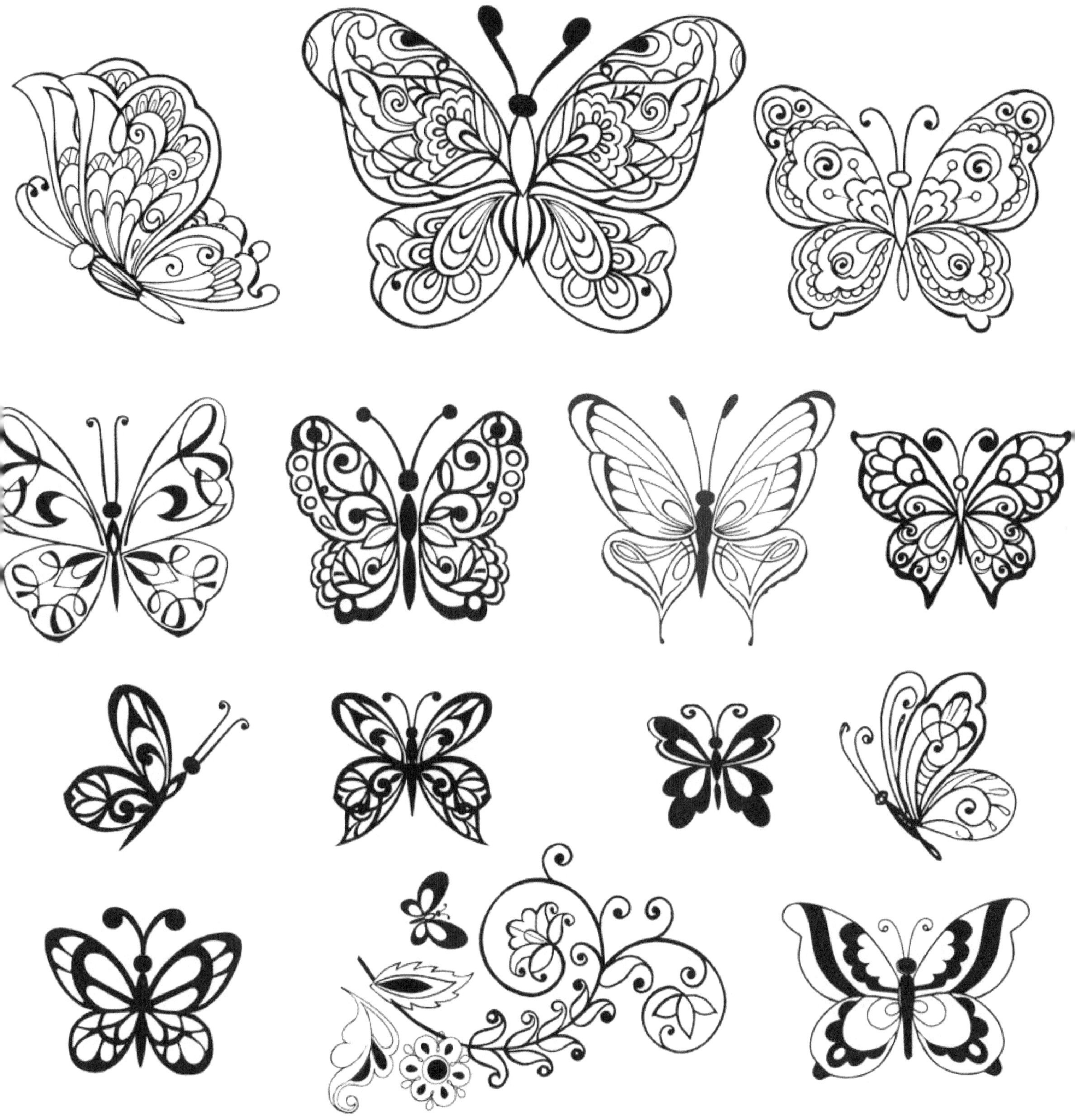

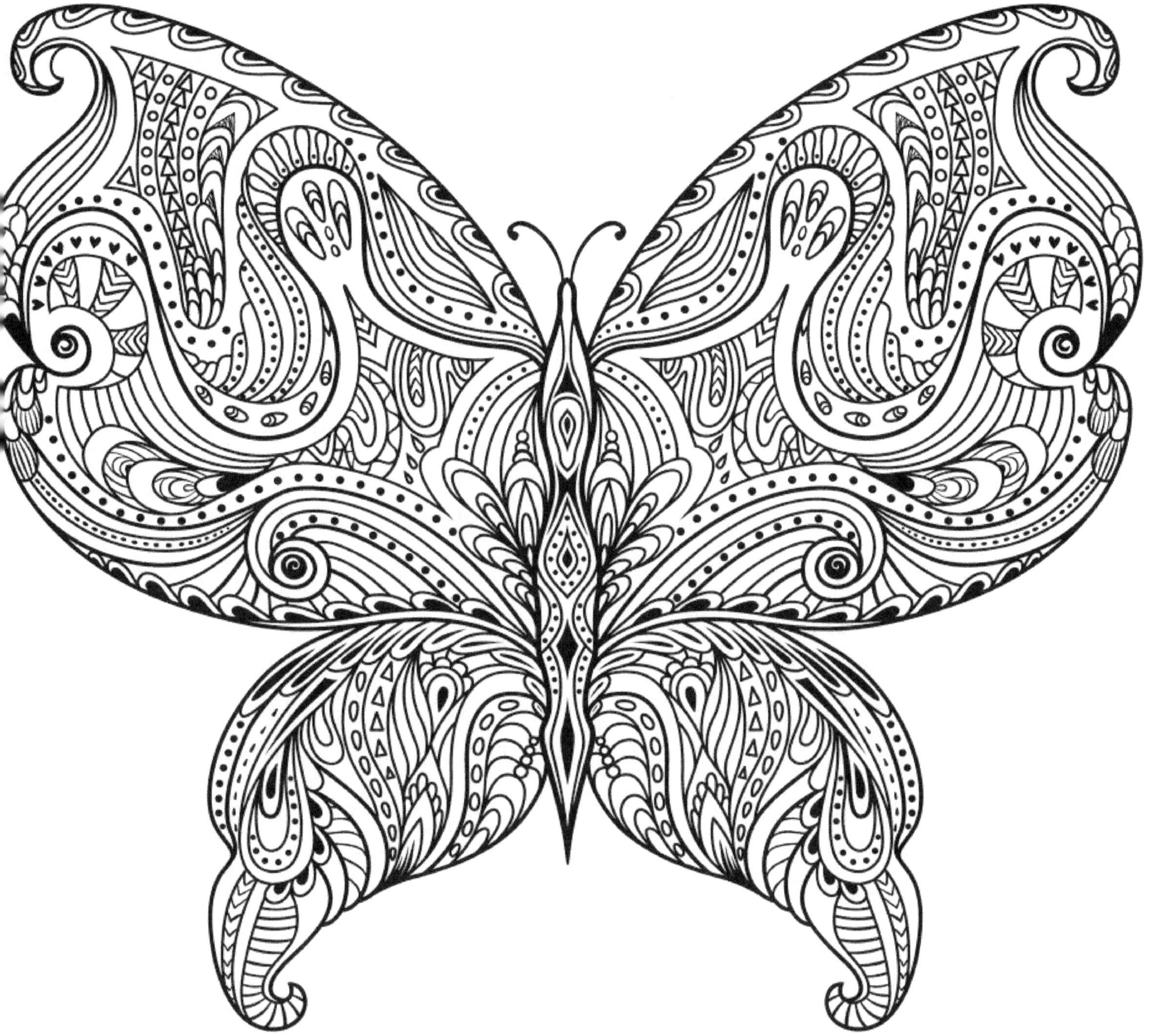

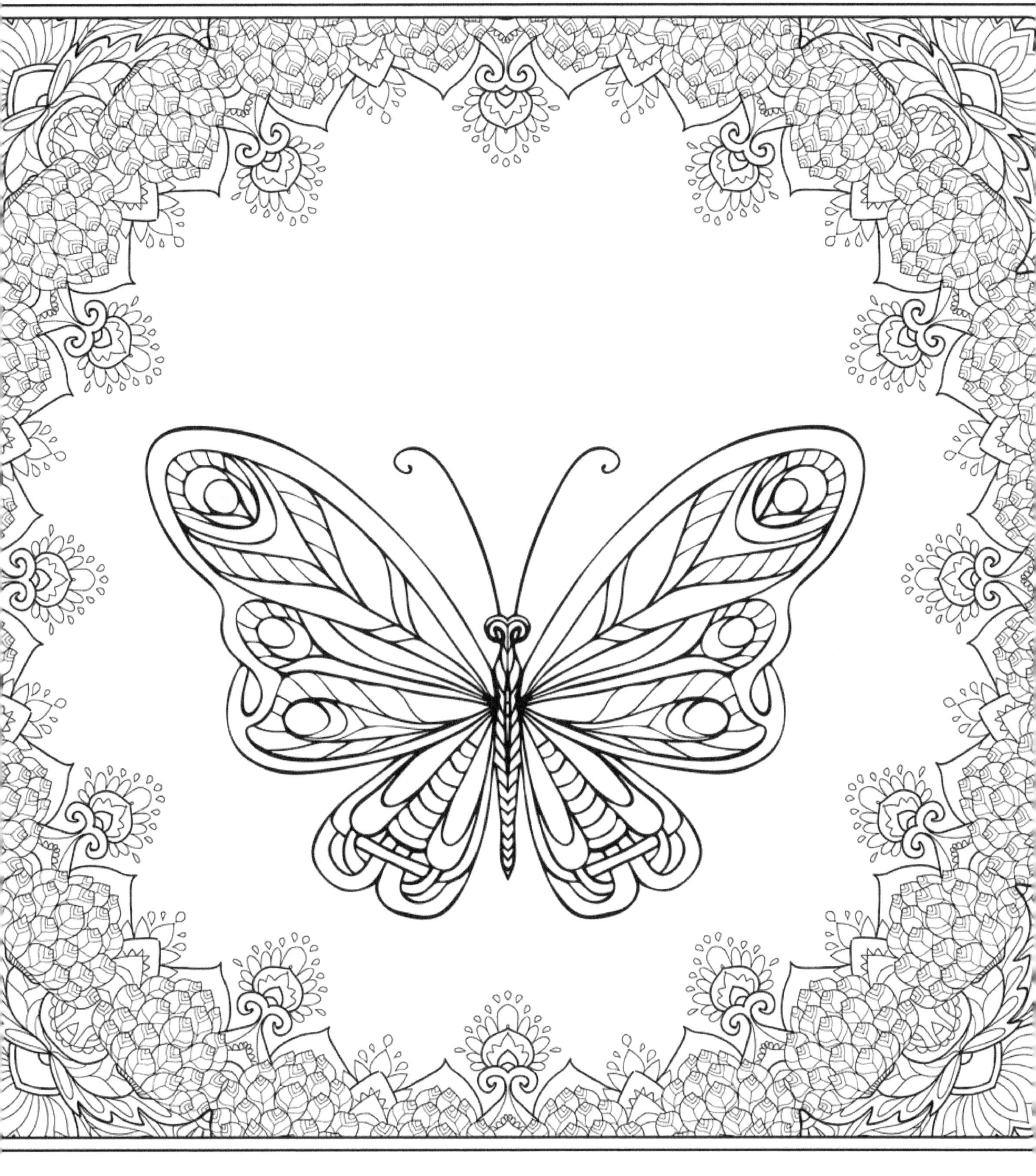

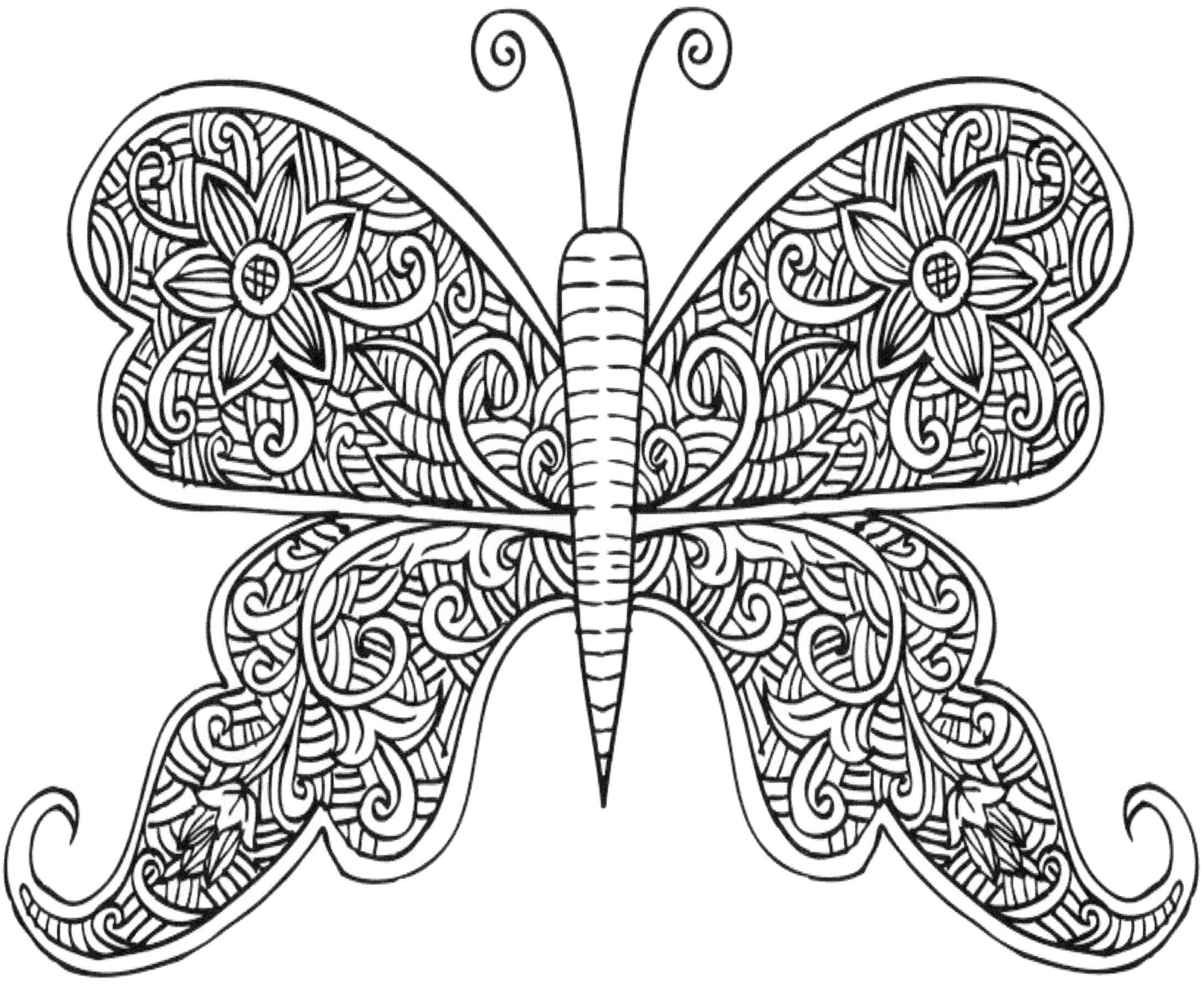

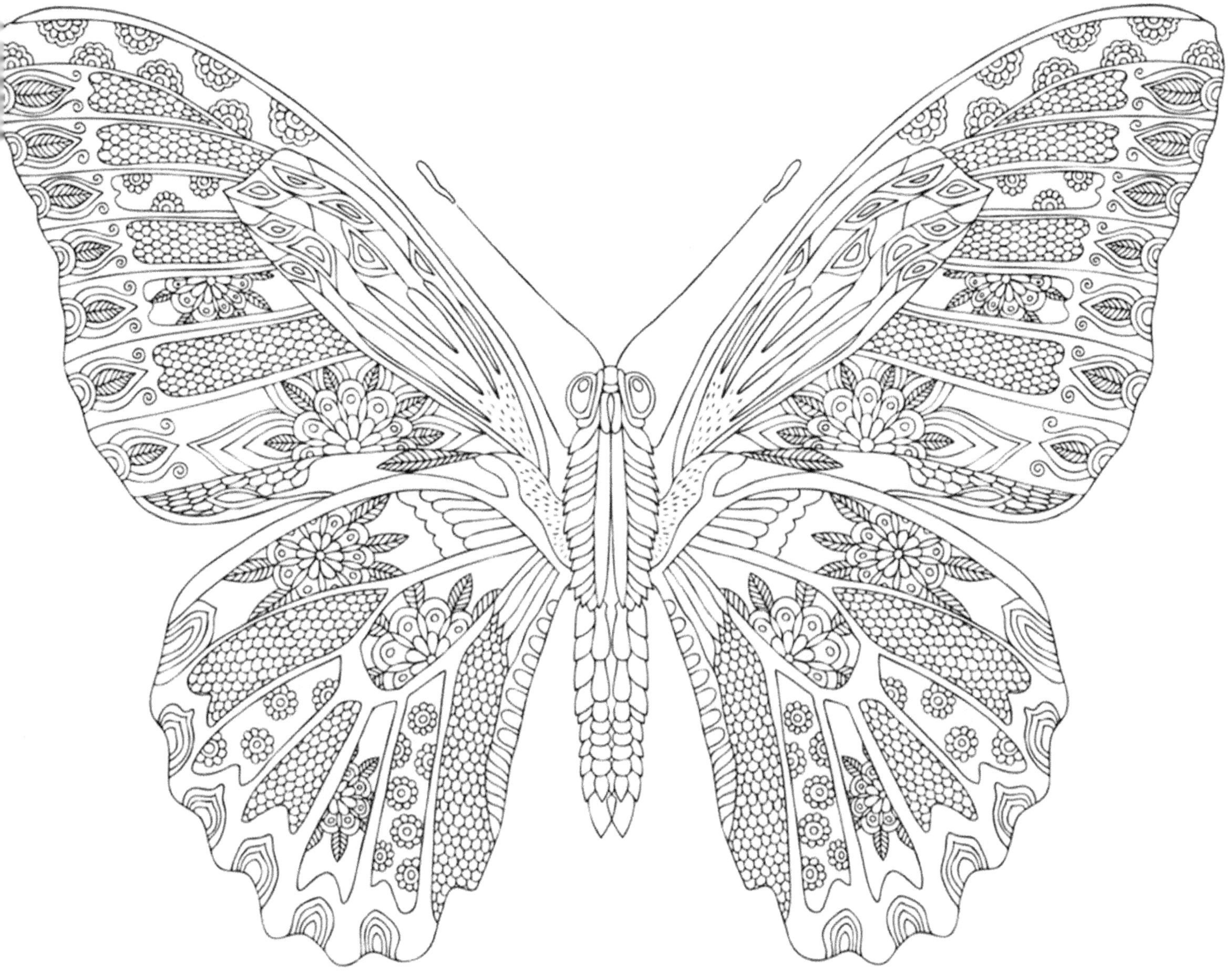

www.ingramcontent.com/pod-product-compliance
Lightning Source LLC
Chambersburg PA
CBHW060002230526
45472CB00008B/1906
* 9 7 8 1 7 1 9 4 7 1 7 8 7 *